PRAISE F[

'Provides an insightful view of Waheeda'—*Times of India*

'Interesting . . . bound to be a winner'—*Telegraph*

'A readable record, especially for fans of the lovely Waheedaji'—*The Hindu*

'The book, very readable and enlivened with several rare photographs, is replete with many other illuminating accounts of Waheeda's work'—*Business Standard*

'Warm, intimate . . . you end up knowing much more than you thought you did about the actress and her time in the film industry' —*Indian Express*

'Exceedingly charming, candid, humorous and disarmingly honest' —*Tribune*

'Insightful . . . Rehman speaks with honesty and humour and *Conversations* is filled with interesting anecdotes'—*India Today*

'Thank God Waheeda decided to do this book and Nasreen Munni Kabir persuaded her where many others have failed. . . . Elegantly produced, with some rare photos, recalling the quiet beauty and professionalism that Waheeda brought to her films'—*Outlook*

'As much a tribute to the eventful life of an exceptional actress as it is a lucid record of a period of moviemaking that set the bar so extraordinarily high that it has rarely been touched since. . . . A veritable treasure trove'—*Tehelka*

'Details previously untold aspects of her life . . . remarkable'—*Vogue*

'A testimony and a very frank account of a celebrity who probably never behaved like one. . . . If you are an ardent lover of good cinema, then you should not miss reading this one'—CNN-IBN

'A fascinating account of a great actor's life'—Anupama Chopra

'An engaging and revealing account'—Rajeev Masand

'Besides delightful behind-the-scenes anecdotes, the book gives us deeper insight into the actress as a person and her relationships with her family, co-stars, mentors and friends from within and outside the film industry. . . . Candid, real and personal'—*Dawn*

'A rare glimpse into the life and career of Waheeda Rehman' —*National*

'There is frankness, honesty and genuine warmth'—*Free Press Journal*

PENGUIN BOOKS

CONVERSATIONS WITH WAHEEDA REHMAN

Nasreen Munni Kabir is a reputed documentary film-maker and writer on films. Based in London, she has made several programmes on Hindi cinema for Channel 4 TV, UK, including the forty-six-part series *Movie Mahal* and *The Inner/Outer World of Shah Rukh Khan*. Her several books are, among others, *Guru Dutt: A Life in Cinema*, *Talking Films* and *Talking Songs* with Javed Akhtar, *A.R. Rahman: The Spirit of Music*, *Lata Mangeshkar: In Her Own Voice* and, most recently, *In the Company of a Poet*, a book of conversations with Gulzar.

CONVERSATIONS WITH

Waheeda Rehman

NASREEN MUNNI KABIR

PENGUIN BOOKS

PENGUIN BOOKS
Published by the Penguin Group
Penguin Books India Pvt. Ltd, 7th Floor, Infinity Tower C, DLF Cyber City,
Gurgaon 122 002, Haryana, India
Penguin Group (USA) Inc., 375 Hudson Street, New York, New York 10014, USA
Penguin Group (Canada), 90 Eglinton Avenue East, Suite 700, Toronto,
Ontario, M4P 2Y3, Canada
Penguin Books Ltd, 80 Strand, London WC2R 0RL, England
Penguin Ireland, 25 St Stephen's Green, Dublin 2, Ireland
(a division of Penguin Books Ltd)
Penguin Group (Australia), 707 Collins Street, Melbourne, Victoria 3008, Australia
Penguin Group (NZ), 67 Apollo Drive, Rosedale, Auckland 0632, New Zealand
Penguin Books (South Africa) (Pty) Ltd, Block D, Rosebank Office Park,
181 Jan Smuts Avenue, Parktown North, Johannesburg 2193, South Africa

Penguin Books Ltd, Registered Offices: 80 Strand, London WC2R 0RL, England

First published in Viking by Penguin Books India 2014
Published in Penguin Books 2015

Copyright © Nasreen Munni Kabir and Waheeda Rehman 2014

Photographs from the collection of Waheeda Rehman unless otherwise indicated.
Frontispiece: a still from *Sahib Bibi Aur Ghulam* (1962). Photograph courtesy: Arun Dutt
Page xvi: a still from *Chaudhvin Ka Chand* (1960). Photograph courtesy: Arun Dutt

ISBN 9780143424031

Typeset in Minion by R. Ajith Kumar, New Delhi
Printed at Replika Press Pvt. Ltd, India

A PENGUIN RANDOM HOUSE COMPANY

This book is dedicated to my wonderful parents who taught me the meaning of compassion and integrity.

—Waheeda Rehman

CONTENTS

ENCOUNTERS WITH WAHEEDA REHMAN

When I was researching the life of Guru Dutt—which ultimately resulted in two books and a documentary made in 1989 for Channel 4 TV, UK, called *In Search of Guru Dutt*—I was naturally very keen to meet Waheeda Rehman. No story about Guru Dutt would have been complete without her speaking of him. She is such a vital presence in his work that when you meet Guru Dutt's fans, you realize that half are in love with him and the other half are in love with her.

Finding a way to meet Waheeda Rehman for my documentary was at the top of my list of priorities. Every time I came to Bombay from London in 1987, I'd try calling her. This was long before mobile phones existed, and getting to speak to a star meant going through a bevy of domestics who answered the phone, all sounding as though they had graduated from the same charm school: 'Madam is not here—call next week—madam is out.'

Out? Out of town?

'*Bahar gaon gayin hai*' [literally translates as 'gone to a village abroad'].

Considering the many calls they take from total unknowns, brushing off yet another stranger must become second nature.

In the middle of 1988, I managed to speak to Waheeda Rehman at last. I explained the reason for my calls and she agreed that I could come and see her the next day, but why a documentary on Guru Dutt? For whom? What would it say? Her hesitation was to be expected because documentaries on Indian film practitioners were rare in those days, and certainly none I knew of were made for a British broadcaster.

The next day I made my way to her house on Bandstand in Bandra. Though her sprawling and gorgeous ground-floor apartment had been rented out, a large room was sectioned off where she stayed during her visits from Bangalore. When Waheeda Rehman opened the door, I was overwhelmed by images of her lifelike screen characters—Gulaabo, Shanti and Rosie. Waheeda Rehman has had such an emotional impact on us all that it took a few minutes for the sheer excitement to settle. Then I explained the purpose of my documentary was to gain insight into Guru Dutt's life and films by recording all the people who had worked alongside him. At that first encounter, Waheedaji was gracious and attentive but not over-friendly—I later realized she is in essence a reserved person. At the end of our hour-long meeting, she agreed to the film interview and we parted.

In Search of Guru Dutt, the documentary, was made later than expected, but Waheeda Rehman had said yes, and, unlike many film stars who make promises they later break, she kept her word and arrived at a friend's flat in Khar where the interview was shot. Waheeda Rehman spoke with life and enthusiasm about the days when she worked with Guru Dutt. She got so involved with that past time that, at one point, she even spoke of him in the present rather than the past tense. During the filmed interview (and in this book) she always referred to him as 'Guruduttji', in deference to his real name. His full name, Gurudutt Shivshanker Padukone, was in fact shortened to Guru Dutt, causing many to assume (and continue to assume) that, since his surname was Dutt, he must be a Bengali rather than a Bangalorean.

I met Waheedaji again in 1990 to film an interview on Lata Mangeshkar, who insisted that this fine actress be part of the documentary I was then making on this great playback singer.

Over the next fifteen years, I met Waheedaji occasionally and gradually got to know her. I found her personal story absorbing. Her father, Mohammed Abdul Rehman, a district commissioner, was from Tamil Nadu. As a young man, he broke with tradition by moving away from his landowning family, preferring to make his life as a bureaucrat rather than live as a rich zamindar. Though not formally educated, her mother, Mumtaz Begum, was by all accounts a woman way ahead of her times. The youngest of four daughters, Waheeda Rehman was a sickly child, suffering from severe asthma. When she was thirteen, her father suddenly passed away and her mother had to somehow make ends meet. Young Waheeda and her sister Sayeeda, both trained in classical dance, performed on the stage, but they earned very little.

Then life changed dramatically for young Waheeda when she accepted a dancing role in the Telugu film, *Rojulu Marayi*. Her sparkling screen presence immediately caught the attention of the audience who instantly fell for her. Her success in the film ultimately led to a meeting with Guru Dutt in Hyderabad. Three months after their fortuitous meeting, in 1955, the seventeen-year-old Waheeda Rehman moved to Bombay where she signed a three-year contract with Guru Dutt Films. The release of *C.I.D.* and *Pyaasa* brought further fame and recognition and, by the end of the 1950s, she was counted among the leading stars of Hindi cinema.

Waheeda Rehman's success was not limited to her performances in Guru Dutt's films. Her subtle screen presence and exceptional dancing talent enchanted the audience. Her natural acting style and willingness to accept atypical roles soon brought her to the attention of India's finest directors. She continued over the years to bring dignity to her characters and substance to her roles, evident in many key films, including *Mujhe Jeene Do*, *Abhijan*, *Guide*, *Teesri Kasam*, *Reshma Aur Shera* and *Khamoshi*. Even in less memorable productions, Waheeda Rehman has made a lasting impression.

In 1974, she married Shashi Rekhy, whose screen name was Kamaljeet. When they became parents to a son and a daughter, they chose to make Bangalore their home, living there on a farm for some sixteen years. Waheeda Rehman stayed away from films, only to return to the screen in the late 1980s, this time in mother roles. But her absence did not diminish the respect and admiration she has won from audiences across generations. Even today, the eyes of her admirers light up when speaking of her.

Besides her personal story, details of which aren't widely known, there is so much cinema history linked to her life that I believed it was important to record her experiences. When I first asked her, sometime in 2005, about writing a book on her, she smilingly said no. Later she revealed to me that she has this habit of saying no at first, even when a film role was offered. Her initial reluctance to the idea of a book came from wondering why her story would interest anyone in the first place. She did not say this for effect. Her humility is genuine. In spite of her great fame, and the countless awards that she has won, including the prestigious Padma Bhushan in 2011, she remains a deeply modest person at heart. In fact she still does not believe that her enduring fame has anything to do with her natural talent, but attributes it all to just being lucky.

Despite her reluctance, I persisted, and made it a point to give her the books I did with others, including Lata Mangeshkar and Gulzar. I wanted her to see that the format of an in-depth conversation might work well and encourage a direct connection with the reader, as she would be sharing her story in her own voice and words. I had almost given up persuading her when, in the summer of 2012, she came to London for a holiday with her friend Barota Malhotra and finally said yes during a meal we were having in Colbeh, a famous Iranian restaurant off Edgware Road.

Between December 2012 and November 2013, we met over twenty-five times in her Bandra home. Our conversations in Hindustani and English were recorded and later transcribed. As many of the film references and times relate to a period prior to 1995, when Bombay was renamed Mumbai, prior to 2001, when Calcutta became Kolkata, and before Madras became Chennai in 1996, I have used the original names of the cities for consistency.

Each of our sessions would last for about two hours. After a few weeks, a relaxed and easy routine set in. I'd ring the doorbell at Sahil, her home in Bombay, and a domestic would open the door and show me into an expansive living room that overlooked the sea—a most gorgeous room dominated by a striking portrait of Waheeda Rehman by M.R. Achrekar. From the living room, I was led to the dining area where I'd set up my MacBook Pro and digital recorder. A minute or two later, Waheedaji walked in, wearing a simple and elegant salwar kameez, smiled warmly, ordered me a nimbu-paani and then we settled down to talk. Her discipline and respect for work showed—she never took calls or sent text messages or allowed anything to interrupt the conversation. Her concentration and attention was total. When lunchtime approached, she would invariably ask me to join her for lunch. Her *tehzeeb* and refined upbringing were always in evidence.

What I discovered about Waheeda Rehman was that she is a feisty lady and has always fought her corner, even from a young age. Besides her confidence and intuitive understanding of right and wrong, she also has a natural gift for storytelling. Admittedly, it takes her time and a sense of trust and ease to open up, but when she does, she comes alive. Her descriptions of the past and the people she knew have a once-upon-a-time feel to them—every event is told with a beginning, middle and end. She has a great memory and gets so involved in evoking the past that her eyes sparkle—it's as though she were seeing actual images of that lived experience. In addition to her lively conversation, her insight into the craft of film-making shows a keen and alert intelligence, allowing this book to hopefully serve as an important chronicle of a great era in Indian cinema.

Getting to know the genuine person behind her illustrious reputation, great beauty and winning smile has been a wonderful privilege. Waheeda Rehman is truly as lovely in real life as she is on the screen.

Nasreen Munni Kabir

My thanks to Sohail Rekhy, Kashvi Rekhy, Arun Dutt, Peter Chappell, Shonali Gajwani, M.A. Mohan, Priya Kumar, Shameem Kabir, Anjelina Rodrigues, Subhash Chheda and the team at Penguin Books India.

WR: My father died in 1951 and for some years after that I saw my mother struggle to make ends meet. The social status, the cars and the houses had gone with his passing and we were left with nothing.

When I turned seventeen, my mother became worried about my future and thought if I were to get married, I might have a more secure life. I didn't want to get married and preferred the idea of working. But what could I do? I didn't have much of an education, so how was I supposed to find a job? It was around that time that the producer C.V. Ramakrishna Prasad, who had known my father, called out of the blue and offered me a dancing role in the Telugu film *Rojulu Marayi*. When I heard about his offer, I jumped with joy and told my mother: 'It is God's wish! Please let me do it.'

My mother immediately curbed my enthusiasm and said it was not a good idea. She thought I was just too young to work in films. She was probably afraid of what people might say, as there used to be a lot of social stigma attached to girls working in cinema in those days. When my father was alive, she could face any sort of criticism, but without his support how would she manage? So she refused Mr Prasad's offer.

But Mr Prasad was a persuasive man. He called back and reassured her: 'Mrs Rehman, I know you come from a decent family, but times have changed. Film acting is as honourable a profession as any other. Your daughter is like a daughter to me and I am producing this film. You can accompany her to the studios and need not leave her side. She has danced on the stage. Where's the harm in her dancing in a film?'

My mother thought about it for a few days and finally agreed. We were living in Vijayawada and because the film was going to be made in Madras, we moved there.

NMK: The dance and song you performed in the 1955 film *Rojulu Marayi*, 'Eruvaka sagaro ranno chinnannaa', became all the rage. I watched the song on YouTube. You have such natural elegance that it is not surprising everyone took notice of you.

WR: I can't tell you how people loved that song. Master Venu composed it and it had a lovely rhythm.

In those days, audiences were known to throw coins at the screen to show their appreciation and that's what people did when my dance started. We were told that when the film was over, people would ask the projectionist to run the song again. My mother couldn't believe it and went to a cinema hall to see for herself—she discovered it was true.

Rojulu Marayi means 'days have changed' and the title perfectly described that moment in my life.

NMK: For a young girl who had no idea of film studios, or how films were made, what was it like facing the camera for the first time? Was the whole process of film-making daunting?

WR: Akkineni Nageswara Rao, Nagarjuna's father, and Shavukar Janaki were the lead stars of the film and I appeared in this one dance scene.

Everything was new to me. I didn't know what to expect. The director Thapi Chanakya helped me get over my nervousness by saying: 'When the assistant holds the clapperboard in front of you to announce the take, pay no attention to it. Don't get nervous. People think they must do something when the take is announced and the camera is rolling—there's nothing you need do. What you're doing is fine.' The director's father was the famous Telugu writer Thapi Dharma Rao who wrote the dialogue for *Rojulu Marayi*.

I remember when I was dancing I kept looking down at my feet because I was very conscious of my uneven, funny-looking toes. People in the south use the term 'Amma' with affection and so Akkineni Nageswara Rao told me gently between takes:

'Amma, don't look down. Look at the camera. You don't have a bad face.'

NMK: Do you remember how long the song took to be completed?

WR: I think it took four or five days. Did you know that a Bombay music director copied that *Rojulu Marayi* song? And guess who? S.D. Burman!

Sometime in the late 1950s, I got a call from Dada: 'You know that Telugu song of yours? Well, sing it for me.'

'Dada, how can I? I am not a singer.'

'I am not going to record you. I know you're not Lata Mangeshkar. Go on, sing!'

I sang it for Dada a couple of times and he composed a song with the same tune for *Bombai Ka Babu. [sings]* 'Dekhne mein bholaa hai dil ka salonaa, Bambai se aaya hai babu chinnannaa.' Majrooh Sultanpuri wrote the lyrics and even used the word '*chinnannaa*' from the original.

Some years later the composer Ravi asked me to sing him the same song because he wanted to rework the tune for a Hindi film as well—I don't remember which film. I told him Burmanda had already used the tune, but Raviji insisted I sing it for him. He thought the song had a beautiful melody.

NMK: The success of *Rojulu Marayi* led to your working in other films in the south. Can you remind us of which ones they were?

WR: The next Telugu film I worked in was *Jayasimha*, in which I played a princess. N.T. Rama Rao was the hero of the film and he was a big star, but did not talk much. Anjali Devi, the heroine of *Jayasimha*, was very friendly with me and told me not to worry. She said he was a reserved man, that's all.

We had to reshoot my 'Eruvaka sagaro . . .' song for the Tamil version of *Rojulu Marayi*, which was called *Kaalam Mari Pochu* and starred Gemini Ganesan. Then I had a dance scene in *Alibabavum 40 Thirudargalum* [Ali Baba and the Forty Thieves], a Tamil film with M.G. Ramachandran in the lead.

I was lucky to have worked with all the leading stars of south India, including M.G. Ramachandran, Gemini Ganesan and N.T. Rama Rao.

NMK: What was it like making films in Madras in the 1950s?

WR: Films were made in a very professional manner. If the call sheet had a start time of nine in the morning, all the actors were there on the dot. I remember there was an excellent Bengali make-up artist who was living in Madras, and the stars would go to his house at six in the morning, have their make-up done and then come to the set at nine, ready to shoot. South Indian actors had a tremendous sense of discipline.

The way of working was different there. If an actor did not behave professionally, or was continuously late for work, no matter how important he or she was—and I have seen this with my own eyes—producers like S.S. Vasan or B. Nagi Reddy

Aged fifteen. Madras, 1953. Photograph: M.A. Mohan.

would throw them out. Not just from the film in which they were starring, but from the industry.

NMK: It sounds like the directors and producers had more clout than the stars.

WR: Yes, they did. Most south Indian films were made within three or four months, and I believe still are, while it sometimes took years for a film to be completed in Bombay. Things have improved a lot. The younger generation of directors today finish a film within a year.

When I began working in Hindi cinema I found films were made in a relaxed—I'd say even slack—way, as compared to the south. In Bombay, the stars came to the set in their own sweet time. When I was shooting for my first Hindi film, I arrived at the studio at eight and was ready to shoot by 9.30. But then I had to sit and wait for Dev Anand who arrived at eleven.

Though I must tell you that if we needed to work late into the evening—because the set was going to be dismantled or something—Dev always agreed to work late. But he never came on time.

NMK: The *Rojulu Marayi* song opened many doors for you and led to your meeting Guru Dutt.

WR: That's right. The film was such a big hit. The cast was invited all around Andhra to celebrate its success and at the end of the tour we arrived in Hyderabad. That's where I met Guruduttji for the first time.

I am a great believer in destiny. Even though Guruduttji did not have the faintest idea who I was, he asked to meet me—a newcomer. It felt like something out of the ordinary—it had to be destiny.

Many good things have happened to me. I never planned anything. Nor did I manipulate or calculate. Yet good things kept happening. Guruduttji happened to be in Hyderabad and I happened to be there too.

NMK: How did he first hear of you?

WR: He was sitting in a distributor's office when they heard a commotion outside—the distributor's name escapes me now—but I think he distributed *Mr & Mrs '55* in Hyderabad. Guruduttji asked him if there was some trouble on the street and he was told the stars of a popular Telugu film were passing by and it was the excited fans that were making the commotion.

The distributor then added: 'A new girl has performed a song in the film. It has caused a sensation. When the stars go on to the stage, the audience demands to see this young girl. Her name is Waheeda Rehman.' Guruduttji was surprised: 'Waheeda Rehman? That's a Muslim name. Does she speak Urdu?'

'I hear she also speaks Telugu and Tamil. She came wearing a *gharaara* and thanked the audience in Urdu at a function where they were celebrating the success of *Rojulu Marayi*.'

Following the success of Rojulu Marayi, *Waheeda Rehman acted in three other south Indian productions. Aged seventeen. Madras, 1955. Photograph: M.A. Mohan.*

That's when Guruduttji told the distributor he would like to meet me because he was looking for new actors to cast in his next production.

The distributor then called Mr Prasad to set up a meeting. Mr Prasad had not heard of Guruduttji. Very few people in the south had heard of him in the mid-fifties. I think there weren't many film magazines at the time and in any case no one in my family read them, so we were unaware of his name.

The distributor explained to Mr Prasad that his friend was a well-known Bombay director and had made a number of successful films. Then Mr Prasad called my mother and told us that Guruduttji wanted to meet me. My mother and I made our way to the distributor's office the next day. I think the meeting lasted about half an hour. Guruduttji hardly spoke. He asked us a few questions in Hindi: where we were from, etc. That was it.

We went back to the hotel where we were staying in Hyderabad. When Mr Prasad asked about the meeting, my mother commented that Guruduttji said very little. Mr Prasad said some people were just made like that. We returned home to Madras a few days later.

NMK: Before Guru Dutt met you, had he seen *Rojulu Marayi*? I say this because I am sure he would have been struck by the sparkling impression you made on the screen.

WR: No, he hadn't seen the film. He had no idea what I looked like on camera. He heard my name and asked to meet me without having seen me at all. There was no reason why the distributor had to mention me in the first place. So how could I not believe it was destiny?

After our first meeting in Hyderabad, three months went by and then someone—I believe his name was Manubhai Patel—came to see us at our home in Madras. He said he was from Bombay. I think he was a film distributor. He said he had come on behalf of the director whom we had met in Hyderabad. Of course, by that time, we had even forgotten Guruduttji's name, to which our visitor said: 'Well, Guru Dutt has asked me to take you to Bombay. He wants to sign you.'

My mother was most surprised and decided to discuss the idea with her friends. They advised her to say Bismillah and go. She was very reluctant. Bombay was like a foreign country to us. As usual she asked Mr Prasad for his advice and he said: 'Go, Mrs Rehman. There's no harm if she works in Bombay, but remember she is not a slave. Don't agree to all their demands. If you don't agree to something, say it. If you don't like living there, come back. Just don't get intimidated.'

So the three of us—my mother, a family friend who was called Mr Lingam and I—landed in Bombay at the end of 1955. We stayed at the Ritz Hotel in Churchgate.

NMK: Did you audition? Or take a camera test?

WR: No audition or camera test. But they took some stills and then the time came to sign the contract. There were a number of people at the meeting—director Raj Khosla who was making *C.I.D.*, in which I was supposed to be cast; production-in-charge S. Guruswamy; cameraman V.K. Murthy, who didn't say much; chief assistant Niranjan and Guruduttji. The meeting was held at Guruduttji's office on the first floor of Famous Studio in Mahalaxmi. Famous had two shooting floors and some offices on an upper floor that were rented to different production companies, including Guru Dutt Films.

One of the first things Raj Khosla said was that my name was too long. It had to be changed. I said: 'My parents have given me this name and I like it. I won't change it.' Pin-drop silence. Raj Khosla got all het up. He was a Punjabi, you know, and they can get all excited. He said: 'Your name is too long. "Waheeda Rehman." Who will say all that? We will call you "Waheeda", and drop the "Rehman". If you don't like it, change your name. It's common practice for actors to have screen names. Dilip Kumar's real name is Yusuf Khan, Meena Kumari is Mahjabeen Bano, Madhubala is Mumtaz Jahan and Nargis is Fatima. Everyone has changed their names.'

I said: 'I am not everyone.'

NMK: You said that?

WR: Yes. *[laughs]*

I don't know how I had the courage, but I didn't stop there and added: 'I have done two Telugu and two Tamil films and did not need to change my name. I haven't run away from home, nor am I hiding from my family. My mother is sitting right here. I am not sure why I should change my name.'

Guruduttji had this habit of sitting with his hand under his chin and his elbow resting on a table. He listened quietly. I was told they needed time to think it over. We stayed on in Bombay for an extra week because my name had become the sticking point.

NMK: I think you were among the first generation of Muslim actresses, post 1950s, who did not adopt a screen name—which was most often a Hindu name. As we know Meena Kumari, Madhubala and Nargis did not use their real names.

WR: Many actors had screen names. I think they wanted my name changed because they didn't think it was sexy. I don't think it was more than that.

I remember every detail of that day. Guruduttji sat without saying a word while Raj Khosla was jumping in and out of his seat.

NMK: Did they suggest any alternative name to you?

WR: They said they'd have to think of one. It was finally agreed at the next meeting that I could keep my own name. They asked my mother to go ahead and sign the contract. I could not sign because I was under eighteen.

Just before she could put pen to paper, I asked her to wait a minute and said: 'I'd like to add something to the contract.' Raj Khosla was surprised: 'Newcomers don't usually make demands. Just sign.' Guruduttji kept silent. Then I told them if I did not like any costumes, I would not wear them. Guruduttji sat up. I am sure he must have thought to himself—here's this girl, not old enough to sign her own contract, and just look at her nerve. [we laugh]

Then he said in his quiet voice: 'I don't make films of that kind. Have you seen any of my films?'

'No.'

'All right. *Mr & Mrs '55* is running in town. Go and see it. We'll talk about the costumes later.'

We were given cinema tickets and we went to see *Mr & Mrs '55* at Swastik Cinema on Lamington Road. The following day we returned to the office. We said there was nothing wrong with the costumes. Madhubala wore sleeveless blouses in the film, but sleeveless blouses were commonplace by then. But I said I still wanted the clause about costumes added. Raj Khosla looked at Guruduttji and said: 'This is amazing, Guru. You're listening to this girl and not saying anything. The choice of costumes depends on the scene and not on the actress.'

I can't believe I was so outspoken, but I insisted: 'When I am older, I might decide to wear a swimsuit. I won't now because I am very shy.' Raj Khosla retorted: 'If you're so shy, why do you want to work in films?' I said calmly: 'I haven't come here of my own accord. You called us.'

No decision was made. We were driven back to the Ritz Hotel. The next day we went back to the office. The clause about my costumes was added and my mother signed my three-year contract with Guru Dutt Films.

NMK: You were amazingly forthright for someone so young. In the 1950s one could not imagine that women could so boldly voice their wishes. And there you and your mother were, arguing about contract clauses without the backing of anyone in the Bombay film industry. You were virtually outsiders to that world.

WR: When my father was on his deathbed, he told us all: 'Fear no one but God. Behave decently and respect your elders. But do not fear anyone.' Maybe those words stayed with me. I was keen to work in films, but I was not dying to.

NMK: It sounds like you were always a confident person.

WR: I think it was because I lost my parents when I was very young. As I mentioned to you, my father died in 1951 when I was thirteen, and I saw my mother somehow manage to make ends meet. Those experiences probably made me strong. I don't know.

Life is full of ups and downs. I have always prayed to God to give me the courage to face problems and not feel defeated.

NMK: Does your faith come from a religious education you had in your childhood?

WR: There was no maulvi saab who came to the house to teach us the Quran Shareef. That was the tradition in many Muslim families. It was my mother who taught us how to pray. My father prayed and kept all the fasts during Ramzan, even though he had to travel about in the heat.

15

My parents encouraged us to live as Muslims, but they were very broad-minded and liberal. Yet certainly we sisters knew we could not cross the line.

NMK: What do you remember of your parents?

WR: They were a wonderful couple. My father was a district commissioner. His name was Mohammed Abdul Rehman and my mother was Mumtaz Begum. She used to wear printed georgette sarees—they were the fashion in those days. Their faces are distinct in my mind, but I cannot recall their voices. I used to call my parents 'Mummy' and 'Daddy'.

My parents believed the most important thing in life was being a good person. My father often said: 'No one has seen hell or heaven. Whatever we have is here—in this life. You must get on with people and be compassionate.'

NMK: You showed me a photograph of your parents. I can see a close resemblance between you and your mother.

WR: My sisters Shahida and Sayeeda look a lot like her too. My eldest sister Zahida looks more like my father who had Tamilian features. I have the same nose as my father.

My maternal grandfather was a tall, fair-skinned man who worked in the police department. Everyone in my mother's family was light-skinned. They were originally from north India—and their ancestors probably came from Afghanistan or Iran. Usually Muslims in the south aren't as fair.

NMK: Did you have a large extended family?

WR: We grew up with many maternal uncles and aunts because my mother had five sisters and four brothers. I don't remember seeing anyone from my father's side. I knew my paternal grandfather was a well-to-do landowner. When my father was born, his mother passed away.

My father used to tell us how keen he was on studying. As a young boy, he would shut himself in his room and put out all the lights. When everyone assumed he was sleeping, he would sneak out of his room through a window and sit under a street lamp and read.

People asked him why he wanted to study—after all he was the son of a rich zamindar and, instead of studying, he should look after the estate like his father had done before him. They told him he could live like a king, but my father was firm: 'I don't want to live like a king. I want to study.' That caused a lot of friction, and when my grandfather remarried he left the family home and settled in Madras.

Father passed the civil service exam and finally became a district commissioner sometime in the 1930s. It was through his friends that his marriage was arranged in the late 1920s. My parents had not seen each other before they got married. After all we're talking about a time that's almost a century ago now. That's how it was in those days.

NMK: Was your mother educated?

WR: Not formally, but she was very intelligent. She was an aware kind of person, and mostly self-taught. I remember she used to read the *Illustrated Weekly*, a popular English-language magazine, and the Urdu edition of the *Reader's Digest*. Since my father was a progressive and modern man, she learned how to play tennis and cards, which was quite unusual for women of her generation.

Most of my childhood was spent in Andhra Pradesh, which was a part of the Madras Presidency then. They were happy times. My father and his friends went deer hunting and the rest of the family went on picnics. We children were given the task of gathering twigs and stones to make a fire for cooking. We were always having parties at home. Because there were only girls in our home, my parents did not want to employ a live-in male cook, and as a result my mother did all the cooking. She was always busy.

NMK: It sounds like you had an idyllic childhood. Did you study in an English-medium school?

WR: Yes. My mother spoke Urdu well and she wanted us to learn how to read and write Urdu. It wasn't easy finding an Urdu teacher in the south, so she taught us herself. But we sisters would dream up some excuse or the other to avoid studying. I did not learn Urdu as well as I should have. I can read but I read slowly.

My father was posted all over south India, so we managed to pick up some of the local languages. I am not very fluent in Tamil and Telugu, but I can get by. You don't easily forget what you learn in your childhood.

NMK: What is your earliest memory?

WR: I have many. But one that stands out?

I must have been about four or five years old. My father was posted to Palghat, which is now called Palakkad. It's in Kerala. During the Onam festival we went to the Palghat Fort to watch the procession of decorated elephants. We stood on the parapet and my father lifted me high in his arms so I could see the elephants through the opening in the fort wall. The image of those beautifully adorned elephants is still clear in my mind.

Like a fool I told my father that I wanted to own an elephant. He said: 'Darling, it's not possible. An elephant is a big animal; you can't keep an elephant as a pet.' 'What about a baby elephant?' He patiently explained that the baby elephant would grow up into a big elephant.

I remember another occasion—in Nagapattinam in Tamil Nadu, a mahout would ride his elephant through our neighbourhood and stop at each house. When they came to our place, we would give the elephant a coconut. It was very smart and would crush the coconut and scoop up the white coconut flesh with its trunk. Animals and birds have fascinated me from a young age.

NMK: Was going to the movies part of your growing-up years?

WR: We saw many films. My parents were fond of music and also enjoyed going to concerts and dance recitals.

Hindi films played in the south a few months after their release, and I believe the first film I saw was *Zeenat* with Noorjehan and Yakub. I must have been about eight years old. How we cried when one of the heroes died! My mother tried consoling us: 'This is all make-believe. He didn't really die.' But we continued wailing in the cinema hall. She tried desperately to quieten us down because everyone was staring at us. She was very embarrassed.

I saw *Barsaat* and *Dastan* when I was about ten. And there was this film with Dev and Madhubala. I don't remember the title. It had a lovely song in it: 'Mehfil mein jal uthi shama parwaane ke liye'.

NMK: It's a song from *Nirala*, a 1950 movie.

WR: *Nirala*? That's right.

NMK: And Hollywood movies? Which ones did you see?

WR: *Gone with the Wind*. There were other films, but I can't remember them now. My parents always made sure the films we saw were suitable for us girls. But more than going to the cinema, our main entertainment was going on picnics.

NMK: I am curious to know if you were influenced by any Hollywood actress when you came to act in films.

WR: I liked Ingrid Bergman very much. You could never forget her presence on the screen. I liked Vivien Leigh in *Gone with the Wind*.

I never wanted to copy any of the Hollywood actresses, and did not think I should perform in the way they did because no one could. Hollywood productions are totally different from ours. How could I do a scene in *Guide* or *Dil Diya Dard Liya* with Vivien Leigh in mind?

I have always believed you should do what you feel is right. I never think: 'Nasreen sits like this so I should sit like her.' You can't imitate anyone.

NMK: You talked about going on picnics as a family. How many sisters are you?

WR: Four. The eldest is Zahida and we call her 'Bi-Apa'. Then there's Shahida, or 'Sha-Apa', and Sayeeda and I. All our names end in 'da'.

When we were growing up, some people commented to my father: 'Rehman, isn't it a pity that God did not give you a son?' He would say: 'Emperor Akbar had nine jewels in his court and I have four.'

I used to get cross when I heard people talk like that. So what if we did not have a brother? I was sure us girls would do well in life.

*Accompanying her father on an official tour (L to R), young Waheeda,
M.A. Rehman, Mumtaz Begum and sister Sayeeda. Circa 1949.*

I once told my father: 'Daddy, don't worry, one day my photograph will appear in the papers. I don't know why, but it will.' I also told him I would own a farm and, many years later, I did. Can you believe that?

NMK: Were these the kind of daydreams you had?

WR: Yes. I had a feeling I was going to make something of my life, even when I was ten years old. But I was a sickly child. I had a kind of allergic asthma and every few months I'd fall ill. My parents were very worried about me and did not know if I would survive. For a while I would be all right and then fall sick again because we kept moving home.

When my father was posted to another city, he usually went on ahead while my mother would arrange for the house to be painted and cleaned before we joined him. She used to call my father 'Saab', and she would say: 'Saab, as soon as you get there, make sure you find a doctor.' She knew I would need a doctor soon enough.

Drinking different kinds of water, the smell of paint, the dust and the new environment would set off an allergic reaction in me. Recuperating from these bouts of illness took time and this meant my schooling suffered a great deal. I was a fairly good student but a slow learner. I can't say I'm very educated in that sense.

NMK: What did the family call you at home? Did you have a pet name?

WR: No. It was just Waheeda. My husband was a Punjabi, and, because I knew Punjabis give their children pet names, when I had children of my own I requested my mother-in-law: 'Mama, please don't call them by some meaningless name like Intu, Pintu, Bintu. Sohail is Sohail and Kashvi is Kashvi.' *[laughs]*

NMK: I believe you started learning Bharatanatyam at a young age. How old were you?

WR: I must have been about nine. We were living in Rajahmundry in Andhra Pradesh. Many cultural events took place there, and we were fortunate to see the great dancer Kamala Laxman on stage. I was completely enamoured of her. She could hold a pose for a long time—statue-like. That's when I told my parents I wanted to learn classical dance.

My first dance guru was Ramachandran. He was a middle-aged man who came to the house to give me dance lessons. I didn't have a lot of energy because of my asthma and, as a result, my lungs were not very strong. My guruji told my mother that dancing might help my lungs expand, and she started regarding the dance lessons as a kind of treatment. In fact they did help. My sister Sayeeda used to play the tabla for me during the lessons but then she started learning how to dance as well.

Three different gurus taught me Bharatanatyam. When my first guru passed away, Tirachandoor Meenaxi Sundaram Pillai became my teacher. That was in Madras and when I moved to

She began studying Bharatanatyam at the age of nine. Seen here at a Madras dance recital.

Bombay, Jayalaxmi Alva became my teacher. They all had their own style.

When I first started learning how to dance some of our relatives were disapproving and told my father: 'Saab, you're a Muslim and you're allowing your daughters to dance?' His reply was: 'Dancing is an art and no art is bad. It's how you conduct yourself that can bring dishonour to your profession. The medical profession is a fine one, but if a doctor misbehaves, you cannot blame his profession, can you?'

NMK: It sounds like your father was a very wise man.

WR: That he was.

NMK: Knowing the stigma against women entering the performing arts, how did you come to dance in public for the first time?

WR: My father was posted to Visakhapatnam, and India's last Governor General, C. Rajagopalachari, who was known as Rajaji, was visiting on an official tour. Whenever dignitaries came to the city, the local officials had to organize a cultural programme. So my father and his team started preparing for Rajaji's arrival. They received a message from Delhi instructing them not to invite artists from other towns and instead favour local talent.

My father and his colleagues were in a flap. How were they going to entertain the Governor General? Daddy's superior told him: 'Rehman, why are you worried? We need a few performers. We have found a violinist and a classical singer and your daughters can dance.' My father said: 'They're young and haven't had enough training.'

'No, they'll be fine.'

When my father came home and told my mother, she was most upset: 'How is it possible? You mean my daughters will dance on the stage? Why did you agree?' He explained that he had tried hard to dissuade his boss, but his boss would not take no for an answer.

The night before the show, my father sat Sayeeda and me down and said: 'Don't be scared. It'll be fine. The stage is always higher than the audience; so don't look down. If you catch someone's eye, you'll get nervous. Look straight ahead and forget about the audience. Do what you can, but do it wholeheartedly.'

Guess what happened the next day? A photograph of Sayeeda and me appeared on the front page of *The Hindu*. Isn't that amazing? *[laughs]*

NMK: Did your father connect it to your daydream?

WR: I don't know.

NMK: The 1940s was a politically turbulent time in India. There was the triumph of Independence in 1947, but also the traumas faced by millions during the Partition. Did your family experience any Hindu–Muslim tension?

WR: No, not at all. In 1947, I was about nine and wasn't really aware of what was going on in the country. But I remember we listened to the radio broadcasts describing the terrible riots in the north and were deeply upset. But there were no riots in the south and as Muslims we never faced any problem.

My father had a doctor friend, an orthodox Brahmin, who told him: 'Don't worry. You can change your name from Rehman to Raman. And if you have any problems, come to my house with your wife and children. You have nothing to worry about. No harm will come to you.'

NMK: Was there any discussion about Gandhiji at home?

WR: Sometimes my father would speak of him. He said he was an amazing man who had achieved so much. It was a terrible shame that things turned out so differently from what Gandhiji had imagined—I mean the violence that erupted.

I recently went to South Africa and visited the house where Gandhiji had lived. I felt very moved to see the rooms where this great man had spent so many years.

NMK: When you were growing up, did you have a sense of the British in India?

WR: My father had many English friends. Around the time of the Partition, he once noticed me staring at a full-page photograph of Lord Mountbatten in the *Illustrated Weekly*. He explained to me that Mountbatten was the last viceroy of India and was leaving India soon. I told him I thought he was very good-looking.

NMK: You said you were thirteen when you lost your father. Had he been unwell for a long time?

WR: No, he was in good health. All of a sudden, he fell ill. He had a very high temperature. The doctors thought it was perhaps typhoid—his fever would go down in the day and up again at night. No one knew what ailed him.

In spite of the fact that he was unwell, he would send for the office files and work at home. We were in Vijayawada at the time. His superior came to the house and scolded him: 'Rehman, what are you doing? You shouldn't be working. Till you get well again, I am appointing another commissioner. All the office facilities are at your disposal, but you must not work.'

But my father wasn't getting better. The doctor told us to take him to the Madras General Hospital, but he insisted on going to Visakhapatnam where he had many friends. The whole family accompanied him there and at first he started feeling much better. Six weeks later, he suddenly collapsed and died. He was only fifty-two. It was such a terrible shock. We were grief-stricken. My mother was a very strong person, but losing someone you cherish is never easy.

NMK: How did she manage after your father passed away? Did she receive a pension?

WR: She did, but it was very little. We had no idea about provident funds and life insurance policies. We hardly had any money. Bi-Apa and Sha-Apa were already married and lived in their own homes. That was around the time Sayeeda and I started dancing on stage. The shows brought in some money, but it wasn't much.

In 1953, two years after my father died, Sayeeda got married and my mother's family migrated to Pakistan. She thought of going with them but did not know what she could do there. She was a heart patient and, because of her fragile health, she became increasingly worried about my future. She was very keen that I marry and settle down. That's when I got the dancing part in *Rojulu Marayi*.

NMK: And as we know that led to your moving to Bombay by the end of 1955 to work in your first Hindi film, *C.I.D.* Dev Anand, who reigned supreme in the 1950s, was the hero of *C.I.D.* in which you played the second heroine, a gentle vamp character called Kamini. Did you find it intimidating to work with the celebrated Dev Anand?

WR: Not really. He was very charming and sweet. When we were introduced to one another, I called him 'Dev Saab'.

He immediately said: 'No, you will call me Dev.'

With Dev Anand in her first Hindi film, C.I.D. *The film was shot at Kardar Studios, Bombay. Circa 1956. Photograph courtesy: Arun Dutt.*

'How can I call you Dev? You are a big star and my senior.'
But he insisted: 'No Mr Anand, no Devji, no Anandji, just Dev.' From that day Dev Saab became Dev.

NMK: You talked about adding a clause in your contract with Guru Dutt Films about the costumes. Did you face any problems regarding what you wore in *C.I.D.*?

WR: There were problems. I had to wear a long skirt with a long-sleeved lace blouse for the song 'Kahin pe nigahein kahin pe nishaana'. In the scene, I sing to distract the villain from finding the hero, Dev Anand, who is hiding in another room. Shamshad Begum sang the song and Bir Sakhuja played the villain.

The problem was the blouse I was given to wear had no lining and I refused to wear it. Raj Khosla was most irritated. The choreographer Zohra Sehgal tried convincing me: 'There's nothing wrong with the blouse. You're just a kid. In the scene, you're trying to seduce the villain.' I said I didn't know anything about seduction, but what I did know was that I had no intention of wearing a see-through blouse. All the assistants and Guruswamy tried persuading me, so did Bhanu Athaiya who designed the costumes, but my mind would not be changed.

Then they called Guruduttji who was writing *Pyaasa* with Abrar Alvi somewhere in Khandala. The phone lines were terrible in those days. Somehow Raj Khosla got through to him and said: 'Your girl is too demanding. She is not coming on the set and Dev Anand is waiting. He has to leave for Switzerland and has no time to waste—you know his wife, Mona, is about to give birth.' Dev's son Suneil was in fact born in Switzerland in June 1956.

So Guruduttji had to return to Bombay and he came to see me in my make-up room and said: 'Raj says you have a problem with the blouse. I don't see anything wrong with it.' I repeated that it had no lining. He called Bhanu Athaiya who told him it would take half a day to have the blouse altered. Guruduttji was worried because Dev had to leave urgently for Switzerland, so I suggested that I wear a dupatta. And that's what was decided. If you see the song 'Kahin pe nigahein', you'll notice I'm wearing a dupatta over the blouse.

Raj Khosla told Guruduttji: 'None of her movies have been

released yet and she is already difficult. If she becomes successful, you'll be in big trouble. Anyway that's your problem.' *[we laugh]*

NMK: Both *C.I.D.* and *Pyaasa* were in production at the same time. You must have been aware of the fact that Dilip Kumar was approached to play the role of Vijay in *Pyaasa*, the role that Guru Dutt finally played. Before you were cast as Gulaabo, Nargis was approached to play the part, and the role of Meena was offered to Madhubala.

WR: It seems Guruduttji did talk to Dilip Saab and warned him that the script could not be changed. Dilip Saab used to sometimes ask for changes. I don't know how far this is true but that's what I heard.

People did tell me how lucky I was to get the role of Gulaabo because both Nargis and Madhubala wanted to play her and neither wanted Meena's role—the role that Mala Sinha played. Maybe they felt Meena was too negative a character while Gulaabo was far more sympathetic.

Because I had a three-year contract with Guru Dutt Films, it was taken for granted that I would act in the films they were producing and that's how I ended up in *Pyaasa*. I wasn't given a narration or anything like that. Maybe I was destined to do Gulaabo's role.

NMK: No one can imagine any other actor but Guru Dutt as Vijay or you as Gulaabo.

C.I.D. was released in 1956 and *Pyaasa* in February 1957. Considering they were made at the same time, how did you balance the shooting schedules?

WR: It helped that both films were being shot at Kardar Studios in Bombay. When I had a few days' break from Raj Khosla's film, I worked on *Pyaasa*. But I gave priority to *C.I.D.* because Guruduttji wanted it released first.

It was on the sets of *Pyaasa* that I first met Abrar Alvi. As you know Guruduttji and Abrar worked together for years.

NMK: How was your early experience of working on Raj Khosla's film? Did you find it difficult?

WR: To be honest I didn't know much about camera angles or framing. If Raj Khosla told me he was going to film a big close-up and I shouldn't move, I would stand as stiff as a board and he would say: 'Why are you rigid? I told you not to move, I didn't tell you to freeze.'

Sometimes Guruduttji would show me the movement and say: 'Don't copy me. I am only explaining the framing. Now you know where to turn and where to look. But do what you feel like doing. I am a man and you're a woman, so don't copy me.'

He was very good at helping newcomers. If they decided to use a 75mm lens for a close-up, Guruduttji would tell me to relax: 'Why have you become like a wooden doll? Whether we use a 50mm, 75mm or 100mm lens, it should not affect you. Just do what is required of you.'

There was an excellent trolley puller called Aziz. Guruduttji was very particular about his trolley shots, so whenever he wanted a trolley shot, the first person he would call out to was Aziz. He pushed the trolley on the tracks so smoothly, and when he stopped you did not feel the slightest bump or the slightest vibration.

NMK: Guru Dutt's trolley shots are his trademark. They're especially fluid in his songs. I am so glad you remembered Aziz's contribution.

Coming back to how you went from the sets of *C.I.D.* to the sets of *Pyaasa*—do you remember the first shot you gave for the film?

WR: It appears at the very end of the song 'Jaane kya tu ne kahi'. Gulaabo enters the courtyard of her house. I hide behind the wall to see if Vijay is following me. That was my first shot. It was filmed at Kardar Studios and later we shot the whole song on location in Calcutta. I think it took three or four days. We worked at night—from ten o'clock to five the next morning. I forget where we were filming, but I remember there were lots of pillars—it was somewhere near the ghats.

NMK: Did you spend much time in Calcutta? I am wondering about the other locations in *Pyaasa*.

This still shows the first shot that she gave for Pyaasa. *Kardar Studios, Bombay, 1956.*

WR: There were some scenes filmed in Calcutta with Guruduttji and Mala Sinha, but I was not needed for those. The scene where Vijay's fans enter a grand hall to commemorate the anniversary of the poet's death was actually filmed on the Asiatic Library steps in Bombay, but it was passed off in the story as Calcutta.

And the song 'Ye duniya agar mil bhi jaaye' was filmed at Famous Studio in Mahalaxmi because they needed a large studio floor. Otherwise most of *Pyaasa* was shot on set at Kardar Studios in Bombay.

NMK: I remember the excellent scene on Park Street in Calcutta where we see the penniless Vijay carrying boxes for a rich seth. The seth looks at Vijay and, under his breath, says something on the lines of: 'What has the world come to? Even the educated are now working as coolies.' And then he hands Vijay a coin in payment. But it later turns out that the seth's coin is counterfeit. The brilliant actor Tulsi Chakraborty who worked with Satyajit Ray plays the seth.

Guru Dutt's son Arun Dutt kindly let me publish a book of his father's letters to his mother. In a letter that Guru Dutt sent to Geeta from Calcutta during the filming of *Pyaasa*, he writes of seeing Satyajit Ray's *Pather Panchali*. Were you at the screening by any chance?

WR: No. As soon as my song was finished, I went back to work with Raj Khosla. But I must tell you he wasn't very happy with my work in his production and had even told Guruduttji: '*C.I.D.* will be her last film.'

After 'Jaane kya tu ne kahi' was shot, the whole unit watched the rushes in Bombay. For some reason I wasn't there that day, but I heard Raj Khosla later commented: 'How is it possible? She is bad in my film and has done such a good job here.'

Guruduttji tried explaining: 'Raj, she is very raw; you need to handle her right. Maybe she did the song well because she is a dancer. She knows how to give silent expressions. She needs a little guidance because she isn't familiar with camera angles. When you use a 75mm lens, she gets very stiff. You have to make her relax.'

NMK: Guru Dutt was clearly more adept at encouraging a good performance from you. Your presence in 'Jaane kya . . .' is imprinted on our minds. It's a brilliant introduction to Gulaabo.

I am thinking of the other *Pyaasa* song 'Aaj sajan mohe ang laga lo' which is a favourite for many. There have been several interpretations of the song's significance. Was it a difficult scene to get right?

WR: Guruduttji must have wondered how to make me convey the right mood. Am I pining for Vijay? What am I feeling?

He knew my father had passed away when I was thirteen and asked me on the day we were going to film the song: 'Did you love your father very much? I am sure you were his pet.'

'Oh yes, I was. I was the youngest in the family.'

He carried on talking about my father. It felt like a casual conversation to me. I didn't realize what Guruduttji was trying to do. *[laughs]*

Then the shot was ready. Just before we were going for a take, he said: 'You miss your father terribly, don't you? When you climb the stairs towards Vijay, just think about your father and how much you would like to go to him. How much you miss him.' That's how he managed to get the kind of facial expression he wanted me to have for the scene.

That's how movies are made. Sometimes the emotions of an actor come from a lived experience. This did not happen often. It was more a question of my imagining how the characters would feel if they were faced with a particular situation.

NMK: Your expression when reacting to the song is perfectly right for the mood and context of 'Aaj sajan . . .'

WR: I have always thought my silent expressions were better than my dialogue delivery. I was hesitant. There were no acting schools in my time and I knew very little about how to modulate the voice.

NMK: Maybe that worked to your advantage because your dialogue delivery has always sounded natural and unrehearsed.

WR: But dialogue delivery had become more natural in my time.

NMK: You're right. It had moved away from a theatrical style of delivery with the new generation of actors who came into Hindi cinema in the late 1940s.

There are many stunning moments in *Pyaasa*—do you have a favourite scene?

WR: I liked the scene when I go to the publisher's office after Vijay is assumed to have committed suicide. I give Mr Ghosh all my savings and ask him to print Vijay's poems.

I also liked the restaurant scene. Vijay hasn't eaten for days and, while he is eating, the restaurant owner asks for money. Vijay gives him the only coin he has. The owner looks at the coin and says it's counterfeit. Vijay is shocked and dismayed— it's the coin that the rich seth had given him on the street. The furious owner asks the waiter to take Vijay's plate away. I am sitting in another corner of the restaurant and, when I overhear them, I stop the waiter and pay for Vijay's meal. I sit at Vijay's table and we talk.

It was a very moving scene.

NMK: And it has such understated and subtle dialogue too— Abrar Alvi at his best. Gulaabo tries persuading Vijay to continue eating, but he is reluctant to accept her charity. As you say it is a very moving scene with poignant and direct dialogue:

GULAABO: *Toh phir khaana kha lo . . . Tumhen meri qasam.*
[Then please eat . . . for my sake.]

VIJAY: *Aap . . . aap apni qasam kyun deti hain mujhe? Aap mujhe theek tarah se jaantein bhi toh nahin.* [For your sake? But you hardly even know me.]

GULAABO: *Khoob jaanti hoon.* [I know you very well.]

VIJAY: *Kaise?* [How?]

GULAABO: *Tumhaari nazmon aur ghazlon se. Jab tumhaare khayaalaat aur jazbaat ko jaan liya, toh ab jaanne ko kya bacha hai?* [Through your poems and songs. If I know your thoughts and feelings—what more is there to know?]

Pyaasa is almost sixty years old and has been screened at festivals all around the world. Its reputation has grown enormously over the years, and it deservedly features in *Time* magazine's list of the best 100 films ever.

Even saying the name 'Pyaasa' stirs an emotional reaction in me, as it must do for thousands of others. What do you think it is about the film that is so moving?

WR: The subject of *Pyaasa* can never date. It's about human values—and the things people seek in life: love, recognition and self-respect.

When the poet, Vijay, gets the recognition he has craved for, he realizes it has no value for him. He has seen that no one bothered about him when he was jobless and penniless,

creenshots from Pyaasa. *Courtesy: Arun Dutt.*

and has understood that importance is given to a man's social standing and not to the person. Meena, the woman he loves, marries Ghosh, putting her selfish needs above love. Greed is everywhere and Vijay's own family is no better, as he finds out that his ruthless brothers are also after the money they can make from his newfound fame.

Some years ago *Pyaasa* was screened in Tokyo, and I asked the head of the Japan Foundation Asia Centre, who had organized the Guru Dutt season there, why he loved the film. He said: 'This is everyone's story. These experiences are beyond national cultures.'

NMK: It is also a film about an artist's place in a materialistic world and the moral choices people make. Vijay's friends and family betray him, and the only people with moral integrity are the poor masseur Abdul Sattar and the prostitute Gulaabo, who is ironically regarded as immoral by the world.

I think *Pyaasa* is among the few Hindi films in which the hero is seen to make a life with a prostitute because usually the prostitute or the hero die by the end of the story so the film can sidestep the associated social stigma.

In Abrar Alvi's book with Sathya Saran, he writes that Gulaabo was based on a prostitute that he personally knew. Do you remember this?

WR: No, not at all. This is the first time I am hearing about it. Abrar never said a word about this to me.

NMK: Many years ago when I was researching my book on Guru Dutt, his colleagues talked about how he had started *Pyaasa*, then scrapped all the scenes and started filming again. The original casting changed too. Johnny Walker was supposed to have initially played Vijay's false friend Shyam, but Guru Dutt thought the audience would not accept Johnny in a negative role and recast him as Abdul Sattar. Many things apparently changed during the production of the film.

Did any of your scenes get cut from the final movie?

With (L to R) actress Shammi, Johnny Walker and Yash Johar.
Bombay, late 1960s. Yash Johar and Shammi remained close friends.

WR: There was a very good song 'Rut phire par din hamaare' that comes in the story in a scene after Gulaabo hears that Vijay has committed suicide. I sing the song, sitting in a boat.

When the final film was ready, we had a trial show and all the cast and crew were there, including Mala Sinha, Burmanda, Murthy and Abrar. As usual, Guruduttji asked for our opinions. My mother and I mentioned that we wanted to say something. Abrar looked at Guruduttji with an expression that said: here's this new girl, what does she know about film-making?

But Guruduttji encouraged us to speak freely. I said I thought my song was very boring. Burmanda sat up and said: 'Waheeda, what are you saying? It's a lovely song.'

'Dada, it's a good song to listen to, but boring to watch. I kept asking myself when it would end.'

NMK: You know, I heard the song on the Net on a site dedicated to Geeta Dutt, and I can guess why the song was filmed in a boat—even though there were no other scenes or songs in *Pyaasa* filmed on the river. Guru Dutt must have chosen a river setting because of a line in the song that says: '*Pahunchi na apni naiyaa ab tak kisi kinaare.*' [My boat has not reached any shore.]

The song is really lovely.

WR: It is, but when Dada thought about it, he also agreed that it did not fit into the story. The hero, Vijay, is assumed dead. Why is Gulaabo singing? The audience would want to know what happens next rather than hear her song. Vijay was supposed to have committed suicide—is he really dead?

There was pin-drop silence after I had made my comment. Mala Sinha turned to me and whispered: 'How can you talk like that? You're a newcomer. You're mad. Why do you want your scene removed?' Guruduttji's great friend Raj Khosla was quick to add: 'This girl knows nothing. Guru, why ask her?'

'No, yaar, they all have a right to say what they think. I even ask my valet Rattan for his opinion. It's okay. Anyway, we're not removing the song.'

My mother and I kept quiet.

You see the whole unit would often eat together during the shoot and my mother would join us. As a result, she and Guruduttji became friends—he called her 'Mummy'. A week after *Pyaasa* was released, he phoned: 'Mummy, I have some news for you. You know the song that you and your daughter did not like? Well, we've taken it out.' My mother got flustered: 'No, there's no need for that.'

Obviously he had not removed the song because of us. He explained: 'In our business, we call a song the audience finds boring a "cigarette song"—that's the moment when people leave the theatre and go out for a smoke. We went to see *Pyaasa* in a theatre and as "Rut phire par din hamaare" began people started walking out. So I have removed it.'

NMK: You were right. A song would have been very intrusive at that moment. Instead there is a fabulous scene. When you hear the news of Vijay's suicide, Gulaabo is distraught and says nothing. She is sitting on her bed with pages of Vijay's poems flying all around her. It's a stunning moment that visually says it all.

The song was removed after the release of the film. That means it was cut out of every print running all over India. How was that doable?

WR: At that time they did not release as many prints as they do now, so it was possible for them to remove the song from every print. When Guruduttji realized the song was slowing the film down, he knew he had to cut it out.

Personally what I like best about *Pyaasa* is that the film is not verbose. That is its great strength. The Urdu dialogue is simple and straightforward. There are no long speeches and lectures. The ideas that Guruduttji wanted to express come through the situations that the characters find themselves in.

NMK: You're right. There is no sermonizing in *Pyaasa* unlike many Hindi films of the period. The political perspective, which gives the film an edge, is not imposed through speeches but is communicated through Sahir Ludhianvi's songs. His Marxist thinking. After all, Guru Dutt had the most brilliant songwriter-poet working in *Pyaasa*.

WR: Ah the songs! Sahir's songs are the pillars of the film. They say everything.

In the 1960s, I remember some of my directors asked me how

the song 'Ye duniya agar mil bhi jaaye' was shot. They tried to film a scene in that style, but it did not work because that song came out of a situation, which worked perfectly in *Pyaasa* and could not be applied to another film.

NMK: Guru Dutt's songs were indeed extensions of the story. Did you ever have any conversations with Sahir Saab during the making of the film?

WR: Not really. He was very quiet and I was quiet too—too many quiet people. *[we laugh]*

I must tell you I didn't make many friends in the early days. I used to read between takes. If I spoke at all, it was to Murthy and Guruswamy. We used to talk in Tamil. It was our secret language. I felt more comfortable talking with them. When Guruduttji saw us whispering away, he would say: 'This is not fair. I don't understand a word.'

NMK: And there was S.D. Burman who gave such extraordinary music to Guru Dutt. Did you get to know him well?

WR: For a very long time I used to listen to *Pyaasa*'s songs at home. I loved S.D. Burman's music. His compositions in *Kala Bazar* were lovely too.

S.D. Burman was such a friendly and sweet man. Everyone called him 'Dada'. When Guruduttji moved his offices to Natraj Studios in Andheri where he shot some of his later films, Dada used to drop by to see us. Dev Anand also shot *Kala Bazar* at Natraj Studios.

It was well known that Dada enjoyed eating paan. He would send his driver to buy special paan from a shop near Bhartiya Vidya Bhavan in South Bombay. He liked sweet paans made with Calcutta leaves and a little *keemam* [tobacco paste]. Guruduttji and Guruswamy also enjoyed eating paan and whenever they saw Dada, they'd ask him for one. He would say: 'Send your car to town to buy paan. My driver has to go miles to buy my stock, so I won't give you any.'

Having refused them, he would turn to me and say with a smile: 'Waheeda, do you want a paan?' Guruduttji and Guruswamy would overhear us and complain: 'We're paan eaters, but you don't give us any. Don't give it to Waheeda; she is about to give a shot and cannot have paan stains on her teeth.'

Dada quietened them down by saying: 'She's a good girl. She'll have the paan and not ask me for another. But, you two? You'll ask for another and then another.' *[laughs]*

NMK: A key character in *Pyaasa* is Abdul Sattar who provided light relief to the melancholic mood of the film—he is the perfect foil to the hero. Johnny Walker is brilliant in this role. Did he improvise a lot?

WR: Oh yes, he added so much to his scenes. If he overdid it, Guruduttji would tone him down. Otherwise Johnny had a free hand.

He was a very serious man in real life—a good person and very serious. Comedy was very loud in those days but Johnny was very different from the other comedians of his time. If he had to do a funny scene or a stupid scene—he performed it with complete sincerity.

NMK: If we could return to the first scene in *Pyaasa*—Vijay is lying on the grass in a park, looking up at the sky. A few lines of a Sahir poem are heard. These were beautifully sung by Mohammed Rafi.

The poem works as a story prologue and describes the poet's view of the world. Vijay sees the injustices around him but is unable to change things.

Ye hanste huwe phool ye mehka huwa gulshan
Ye rang mein aur noor mein doobi huwi raahen (x2)
Ye phoolon ka ras pi ke machalte huwe bhanware (x2)
Main doon bhi toh kya doon tumhen ae shokh nazaaro
Le-de ke mere paas kuchh aansu hain kuchh aahen.

[These smiling flowers, this fragrant garden,
These paths bathed in colour and light. (x2)
Drinking the nectar of the flowers, the bees sway. (x2)
What can I give to you, O splendid nature?
All that I have is a few tears, a few sighs.]

Guru Dutt's portrayal of Vijay is utterly heartfelt and that's probably why audiences see no distinction between the character of Vijay and Guru Dutt himself. There is a blurring of the two personalities in our minds. Do you think Guru Dutt was like the melancholic Vijay in real life?

WR: To be very honest with you, when we were making *Pyaasa* I was only eighteen. I didn't study Guruduttji as a person. It was my second Hindi film and I was very involved with my work.

But he was a very quiet person—constantly thinking about films. All of a sudden, he would ask me if I had read such and such book, a book that he had thought of adapting for the screen. When I was sitting with him and, say, a third person was around—Murthy or Guruswamy—and we started talking, we could sense that Guruduttji would not be listening to us. He was lost in his own thoughts. When we turned to him, he had even forgotten how the conversation had started. If you looked into his eyes, he was often not there.

If anyone asked me what he loved the most in the world, it was his work. His work came first then his wife and children. He was obsessed with film-making.

NMK: Did the reactions to *Pyaasa* meet his expectations?

WR: Oh yes! Everyone had their doubts about the film doing well. I myself had no idea if audiences would like it. But *Pyaasa* picked up gradually. People loved it and especially loved the music. It ran for twenty-five weeks.

NMK: With the release of *C.I.D.* and then *Pyaasa*, you became very well known. Do you remember the first day you were recognized on the street?

WR: Not really, but I do remember an incident during the making of these films. In those days, you could hire a victoria [a horse carriage] and ride along Marine Drive and I remember telling my mother: 'Mummy, before my movies are released, let's go for a ride in a victoria because I won't be able to do it later.' But we didn't go for the ride and soon I forgot about it.

A few days later, I noticed that my mother was not talking to me. She didn't keep very good health, and so I asked her if she was all right. She told me there was nothing wrong with her, but refused to say much else. Finally she explained why she was upset with me: 'You wanted to ride in a victoria because you said you couldn't do it after your films were released. I think all this has gone to your head. What will happen to you later?' I understood what she meant and apologized to her.

NMK: Were you ever mobbed?

WR: I was recognized but not mobbed. When *C.I.D.* and *Pyaasa* celebrated their silver jubilees, I did become very popular. But stars did not have as much exposure as they have today. There were only a few film magazines like *Filmfare* and *Screen*, and people were largely unaware of how we actors looked off-screen. Now you open any newspaper and you see whole sections dedicated to movie stars. The stars today have lost the freedom that actors of my generation had. We could go out without any major problem.

NMK: It is ironic to think that *Pyaasa* did not win any awards, and all the 1958 Filmfare Awards went to *Mother India*.

WR: Was *Mother India* released in 1957? I forget.

I was in fact nominated for a Filmfare Award for *Pyaasa*. J.C. Jain, who started *Filmfare* in 1952, called to congratulate me and said: 'You are a very lucky girl; you have been nominated in a supporting role.' I was very pleased that people had liked my work. Then it seems he told Guruduttji, who said: 'She is not playing a supporting role. Her role is equal to Mala Sinha's. She is my second leading lady.'

J.C. Jain explained: 'Mala Sinha is her senior and a big star. This is only Waheeda's second movie.'

'In that case, I won't let her accept the nomination.'

I was a little disappointed but later understood why he felt that way. Guruduttji didn't want me to be considered a secondary heroine.

NMK: You were contracted with Guru Dutt Films for three years. What were you earning?

WR: My starting salary was 2000 rupees a month, and later it was increased to 3500. It was a lot at the time. Some actresses of my generation were earning between 500 and 1000 a month.

For *Solva Saal*, my first film as a freelancer, I received 30,000 rupees. The highest I ever earned in my career was 7 lakh for a film.

NMK: When did you manage to buy your first car?

WR: It was Geeta who picked up my mother and me in her car to attend *C.I.D.*'s premiere. The very next day, I told my mother: 'We shall go in our own car for *Pyaasa*'s premiere.'

I wasn't earning a lot of money and thought we could perhaps get a second-hand car. Guruswamy suggested we buy one on instalments. For *Pyaasa*'s premiere we did manage to go in our own car—a convertible white Dodge. It was the first car that I managed to buy.

NMK: There was a two-year gap between the release of *Pyaasa* and *Kaagaz Ke Phool* in 1959. How did you come to do *Solva Saal* in the meantime?

WR: Guruduttji was a very fair person, and even though I was not supposed to accept any outside work, he called my mother and said there was this film that Raj Khosla was making with Dev Anand, and I should do it. My mother brought up the issue of my three-year exclusive contract and he said: 'Mummy, girls have a very short screen life as lead heroines. When they get married, it's all over. I don't mind her working with other directors. But whenever I start a movie, my shooting dates must be given priority. Anyway, you know, Dev and Raj Khosla are part of my team.'

If I was ever offered a role, my mother first discussed it with Guruduttji. When H.S. Rawail came to talk to us about *Roop Ki Rani Choron Ka Raja*, it was Guruduttji who said I should go ahead. We didn't know H.S. Rawail. My mother and I knew only the big names of cinema like Sohrab Modi and Mehboob Khan. I believe she had seen *Dr Kotnis Ki Amar Kahani*, and so had heard of V. Shantaram.

NMK: Both your Hindi film releases were commercial hits and critically acclaimed films, especially *Pyaasa*. So 1957 was a joyful year for you, but in the same year you lost your mother. Can you tell me what happened?

WR: While I was working on *Solva Saal*, my mother would accompany me to the studio. She started to feel poorly and decided she should rest at home. I called my sister Sayeeda who was living in Vijayawada and asked her to come to Bombay at once. I was shooting all day and did not want my mother to be alone at home, given the fact she suffered from a heart condition. Sayeeda came to Bombay as soon as she could. She was a few months' pregnant at the time.

One day my servant called me at the studio and asked me to come home immediately because my mother was feeling very ill. I rushed back and found her barely conscious. We panicked and rushed her to Northcote Nursing Home, which was close to our Colaba house.

My mother had suffered a massive stroke. The doctors gave her an injection and, thank God, she recovered. When she regained consciousness, we found the stroke had affected her speech and so she spoke with difficulty. She had to stay in the nursing home for six weeks. My elder sister Sha-Apa came to Bombay from Madras to be with us. When my mother returned home, she started improving, but it took her three months to regain normal speech.

Some weeks later, Sayeeda was due to give birth to her third child. We admitted her into the same nursing home where my mother was treated. Sayeeda had a difficult delivery and on 9 December 1957 her son was born. When my mother saw the baby, she was very happy. She took the child in her arms and said: 'I am going to call him Ashfaq.'

I had no shooting for three days and my mother and I would go and see Sayeeda every day. Three days after Ashfaq was born, on 12 December, we were sitting with Sayeeda and her baby when my mother said: 'Waheeda, I am not feeling very well. I'll go and see the doctor. You'll be shooting from tomorrow, so stay here with your sister. There's no need to come with me. I'll go to the doctor's and come straight back.'

Fifteen minutes later, our driver came running into Sayeeda's room and said: 'Mataji did not see the doctor, but decided to go home. She isn't at all well. Hurry.' I ran back home.

My mother was lying on her side. I turned her around so

that I could see her face. I kept calling out to her: 'Mummy, Mummy!' She was very still. I told the cook to get the doctor who lived nearby. The cook returned with the doctor who said: 'She is not my patient. There's nothing I can do.' I told him it was an emergency and he had to help her until her cardiologist, Dr Vakil, could come from Opera House. He said: 'There is nothing I can do. She has passed away.' I got very angry with him and said: 'What nonsense! Just give her an injection. She'll be all right.' But he did not listen to me.

Although the nursing home was nearby, Sayeeda was weak and could not come home till later that afternoon. I didn't know many people in Bombay. I was still more or less a stranger to the city, and so I called Guruduttji and told him to send Guruswamy at once. Guruswamy arrived and he was followed by Guruduttji and Murthy. I could not get through to Dr Vakil, but another doctor came in his place. He examined my mother and said she had passed away an hour earlier. I was completely shocked and refused to believe him. It was too much for me to take in.

Guruswamy asked for my elder sisters' numbers so he could call Bi-Apa and Sha-Apa who were back in Madras by then. Since I am a Muslim, Guruduttji thought I should have some older women around me as they would know what had to be done. He called Mrs Mehboob Khan and Mrs A.R. Kardar and very sweetly they came over. I was dazed and shocked and couldn't even cry. What irritated me was hearing them say: 'Look at this girl. She isn't even crying. She looks fine.' I thought to myself: why did they come? I was so upset that I became angry with them for no reason.

I kept going into my mother's room and touching her. I pulled the sheet away from her face. She was still warm. I kept asking everyone why the doctor hadn't come. Why weren't they giving her an injection? I had once heard that when a person dies the body turns cold, and since my mother felt warm to the touch, I could not accept that she had passed away.

Guruswamy called the actor Rehman, thinking he would know about Muslim burials because neither Guruswamy nor Guruduttji knew anything about our customs. Rehman Saab lived nearby in Colaba and came over immediately. At eight that evening they took my mother away.

NMK: You were only nineteen. You must have felt very alone.

WR: Those were terrible days. Despite the fact that Rehman Saab was a bachelor at the time, he sent food for us for the next three days. People in mourning are not in a state of mind to worry about cooking and all that, and so it is customary that friends or family send food. Many visitors dropped by to offer their condolences and we had to have something to offer to the guests who came.

NMK: How did you cope emotionally?

WR: For a year after that, almost every night, I had a very bad recurring dream. I dreamt that my mother had not died and I kept asking if I had buried her too quickly without being sure that she was dead. Had I rushed? The doctor hadn't come. She was not breathing, but then why was her body still warm? It was a terrifying nightmare.

My father had gone and now my mother. My sisters were married. I felt all alone in the world. I was totally confused. I didn't know what to do. Should I continue working or go back? But go back where? To whom? I didn't want to live with my elder sisters. They were married and had their own families to look after. I didn't know what to do.

People said the best thing for me was to carry on working and finish *Solva Saal* and *Roop Ki Rani Choron Ka Raja*. They said I was lucky because at least I had work. It was the best remedy under the circumstances.

NMK: How did you manage the shooting of *Solva Saal*?

WR: After my mother passed away, Sayeeda stayed on in Bombay with her family and ran the house. Our old friend Mr Lingam came from Madras and he looked after my accounts. He was a very sweet and kind man.

Raj Khosla, Dev and his assistants were very kind to me on the sets of *Solva Saal*. They distracted me, talking about this and that. Dev was very caring and kept comforting me, saying: '*Kaam karo. Aur kya karogi?* [Carry on working. What else can you do?] Your sisters are married, and besides, it's not the same thing to live in a married sister's home. By God's grace, you have two movies—finish them and then decide what you want to do.'

NMK: How old was your mother when she passed away?

WR: She was about forty-nine. Not even fifty. She was very young, you know.

I always believed my mother brought me to Bombay to leave me in the world of films. If she had not done that, I doubt I would have had the courage to move here alone.

NMK: In your next film, *Kaagaz Ke Phool*, your feelings of personal loss are quite visible. I am thinking of the scene where Suresh Sinha and Shanti decide to separate and not see one another again. Your face is full of sadness. The loss of your mother must have been on your mind.

WR: I was very sad and upset. I felt alone. It was a difficult time. But I always had a sense of discipline and made sure I got to the set on time and did what was required of me. I had to put aside my personal feelings when it came to work.

NMK: *Kaagaz Ke Phool* was the first CinemaScope film made in India. Do you remember any discussions about the planning of it?

WR: I was never involved with those kinds of discussions. When we actors finished the day's shoot, I used to run out of the studio like a schoolgirl let out of class! Guruduttji, Murthy, Abrar and the technical team then sat together and discussed production issues.

NMK: *Kaagaz Ke Phool* is now considered an important classic but at the time of its release, the reviews were pretty dismal. Some people felt the story was confused.

WR: It was. When we saw the trial show, I personally didn't think the audience would like it. Abrar Saab got very angry with me and said: 'What do you know? Why are you saying that?' I thought the film was too sad and there wasn't enough happening in the story. It was too heavy.

As I said earlier, Guruduttji had this habit of asking his cast and crew what they thought about a film, and he also made it a point to ask his valet Rattan. Some people were taken aback by this and would say: 'What does your valet know? Why ask him?' But he believed Rattan's reaction would not be different from that of the audience.

When Rattan saw *Kagaaz Ke Phool,* he said: 'I hope you won't get upset, Saab. But Johnny Walker's part is not interesting, it isn't funny.' And he was right.

NMK: I agree. Johnny Walker's subplot stopped the narrative flow and weighed the whole story down.

WR: So Rattan was right, you see? Guruduttji told us that *Kaagaz Ke Phool* was inspired by *A Star Is Born*.

NMK: You mean the 1954 musical with James Mason and Judy Garland? One can see similarities in the story. A star played by James Mason falls in love with a showgirl (Judy Garland). She becomes famous while the career of the male star declines. He turns into an alcoholic and finally commits suicide by walking into the sea. Basically it's the story of the rise of one artist and the decline of the other.

Today *Kaagaz Ke Phool* is a great favourite for many and has gained the reputation of a classic. But I have to admit I have great reservations about the film despite it having some deeply moving scenes. Undoubtedly, Murthy's photography is ingenious, especially in the song 'Waqt ne kiya'. This most gifted cinematographer once explained to me in an interview how he created the lighting effect.

He used two large mirrors—one was placed on the roof of the Mehboob Studio floor where the song was filmed, and the other was positioned on the catwalk inside the set. When sunlight fell on the first mirror, Murthy redirected it to the second mirror and from there he managed to create two parallel beams of light that flooded the set.

WR: That was a wonderful scene. It was something that had never been seen before. I know there are many good moments in *Kaagaz Ke Phool*, but as a whole I didn't think it worked.

I thank God it is considered such a classic today. But I can't help feeling the story has flaws.

NMK: Guru Dutt and V.K. Murthy created brilliant cinema together. They must have had a fabulous understanding and closeness between them.

WR: Yes, they understood each other very well, but fought a lot. When Guruduttji explained a shot he wanted to Murthy, he wanted the shot ready at once. But they were never simple—they often involved complicated angles, trolley movements, close-ups, mid shots, etc. And since Guruduttji was already thinking about what he wanted next, he would get impatient and say: 'Murthy, yaar, are you ready? Hurry up now!'

'*Nahin, Guru, abhi to shuru kiya maine.*' [I have just started.]

'Arey yaar, you're taking a lot of time.'

'It hasn't been five minutes since you told me what you wanted. The camera is not in position. How can the lighting be ready?'

Murthy Saab would storm off the sets while Guruduttji sat quietly. No one in the unit would utter a word. Then Guruduttji would ask his chief assistant: 'Did I say too much? What shall I do?' When Guruswamy became more familiar with him, he'd tell him: 'I think you should go and say sorry.'

Guruduttji would disappear and a few minutes later he returned to the sets with his arms around Murthy: '*Murthy,*

(L to R) Unidentified assistant, Guru Dutt, boatman, S. Guruswamy
and V.K. Murthy on a recce in Bengal. Early 1960s. Photograph
courtesy: Late Tarun Dutt.

yaar, main aisa hi hun.' [Murthy, my friend, that's just me.] It was very sweet to watch them arguing like children.

NMK: The sets of *Kaagaz Ke Phool* were superbly designed by M.R. Achrekar. His contribution to Indian cinema of the fifties was tremendous. He was also a fine artist and painted a stunning portrait of you. How did that come about?

WR: We were travelling together on a flight to attend the Delhi premiere of *Kaagaz Ke Phool*. I was sitting in the row ahead of Achrekar Saab. He came over to me and asked if he could sketch me during the flight. Of course I had no objection. Between Bombay and Delhi, he made twelve pencil drawings and when we landed in Delhi, he said he'd like to paint a portrait of me. He asked whether I would go over to his house in Shivaji Park and we exchanged phone numbers. When I returned to Bombay, I went over to his house some weeks later.

We had two sittings of an hour each. This was sometime in 1961. He drew five or six sketches and then painted the portrait. He worked very fast. It was amazing. When the portrait was ready, he called his wife to have a look at it. She stared at the painting and then at me and said: 'It's very good but the mole on her upper lip is missing.' She was so observant. Then Achrekar Saab made a second portrait that he gifted to me.

I have cherished his painting and it has hung on the walls of the many homes I have lived in. I have it here with me in Sahil. Achrekar Saab was such a simple and lovely man. One day I

Celebrated artist and set designer M.R. Achrekar painted this portrait in the early 1960s. Poonam Apartments, Bombay.

must try and buy the other portrait he made of me—the one with the missing mole.

NMK: He drew brilliant sketches of Guru Dutt and Raj Kapoor. And I have seen his beautiful paintings of Lata Mangeshkar, Meena Kumari and Nargis. He managed to capture the inner life of these stars, including you. M.R. Achrekar was a formidable talent and that's obvious in all his work, including his set designs.

After *Kaagaz Ke Phool*, the next film that Guru Dutt produced and released in 1960 was *Chaudhvin Ka Chand*. I am wondering why he didn't direct it?

WR: He believed that Sadiq Saab, being a Muslim, would know the nuances of Lucknavi culture. Little subtle details. For example, when Jameela—the character I play—gets flustered, she says: 'Hai Allah!' She would say this and immediately cover her head if a stranger happened to enter the house. It's these delicate touches. Sadiq Saab was familiar with Muslim traditions and etiquette. Guruduttji had made the right decision. He helped with the filming of the songs, of course.

When Guruduttji was producing *Chaudhvin Ka Chand*, people asked him why he had chosen a director whose recent films were flops. He said Sadiq Saab may be down and out, but that did not take away from his directing abilities. Guruduttji was a very generous man by nature and even sent Sadiq Saab provisions for his house because he knew he was going through difficult times.

NMK: V.K. Murthy told me he went to London as an observer on the sets of *The Guns of Navarone* because Guru Dutt had asked him to learn about colour photography so he could reshoot the title song 'Chaudhvin ka chand ho' in colour, even though the rest of the film was photographed in black and white by Nariman Irani.

Why the need to redo the song?

WR: By the early 1960s, many Indian film-makers had started making song sequences in colour, if not shooting whole movies in colour. We were, however, nearly halfway through our production. When *Chaudhvin Ka Chand* became a super hit, Guruduttji decided to reshoot the song in colour because he knew people would go back to see the colour version since the song was so popular. It was a kind of gimmick.

I remember I had to dip chamois leather in an ice bucket and apply it to my face because the lights burned my skin. The lights were terribly hot. The colour version was the same as the original, shot by shot. We reshot it at Natraj Studios.

The Censor Board wanted the song re-censored and asked us to remove a close-up where I am seen turning my face towards the camera. They said my eyes looked too red and sensual. Guruduttji said my eyes were red because of the strong lighting and explained the characters were husband and wife, and so where was the problem? If the Censor Board members of that era saw the films of today, I wonder what they would say. *[we laugh]*

Chaudhvin Ka Chand is a lovely film. The story of sacrifice between the two friends Pyare Mian [Rehman] and Aslam [Guru Dutt] is very moving.

NMK: It's a wonderful film. Rehman was excellent, and equally good as Mr Ghosh in *Pyaasa* and Chhote Babu in *Sahib Bibi Aur Ghulam*. He is a hugely underrated actor.

WR: Many people have asked me if I was related to Rehman Saab because of our surnames. After the release of *Pyaasa*, my mother and I were invited to a number of parties. Rehman Saab was very protective of me and would quietly come and tell us to leave because everyone was drinking and the food was bound to be served very late. He could tell that my mother and I were out of place. Sometimes Rehman Saab asked the hostess to give us dinner in another room. He would advise us to eat and leave discreetly so we did not have to say goodbye to everyone.

I remember Rehman Saab wasn't comfortable with dialogue lines that started with a 'k'—like the words '*kab*' or '*kyun*'. He would get stuck, and so Guruduttji would ask Abrar to change the line. Guruduttji always found an alternate way of expressing the same mood or feeling. He did not think there was only one way of making a scene work.

Rehman was a very good actor, and after *Pyaasa* he was in great demand for character roles. Like Raaj Kumar, he had a wonderful personality and although they both played lead roles, I think they had greater presence as secondary heroes.

NMK: Did you know *Chaudhvin Ka Chand* was based on a story by Saghar Usmani called 'Ek Jhalak' [A Glimpse]?

WR: I didn't know that. Sometime in 1982 or '83, Rajesh Khanna wanted to remake the film. He asked me to see the film again on video. I said I didn't have a VCR or a television. He was shocked. We even discussed a possible cast, but he didn't pursue the idea.

NMK: I don't think certain films should be remade.

WR: I agree. No one would dare remake *Gone with the Wind*.

Ek Phool Char Kaante was remade with Salman Khan and Karisma Kapoor, but it didn't do well. Pritish Nandy was thinking of remaking *Sahib Bibi Aur Ghulam*. But the idea was shelved. There was a TV serial based on *Sahib Bibi*. It wasn't very good.

NMK: Unfortunately you do not have any scenes with Meena Kumari in *Sahib Bibi*, the Guru Dutt film that came after *Chaudhvin Ka Chand*.

WR: I wanted very much to do a scene with her. When I asked Guruduttji to work a scene into the story, he said the two women do not meet in the novel. I immediately told him: 'When I question you about something, you tell me film-makers must have artistic licence, so why not create a situation?' *[laughs]*

Jabba keeps asking Bhoothnath about Chhoti Bahu. She is curious about her and I suggested that Bhoothnath could take

Jabba to the haveli so she could see Chhoti Bahu, at least from afar. Guruduttji hummed and hawed and finally said he didn't think it would work.

NMK: Did you go on set while Meena Kumari was shooting?

WR: I did once. They were filming the song 'Na jao saiyyan chhuda ke baiyan'. Guruduttji was there, even though he was not required for the scene.

By the time we were making *Sahib Bibi*, I had made friends with many people in films. I was ten years younger to Meenaji but we were good friends. When she left her husband Kamaal Amrohi, I suggested she buy a flat in the building where I was living. I thought we could help each other, and so she needn't feel alone. When I heard she was very ill, I immediately went to the nursing home where she had been admitted. It was somewhere in Chowpatty. She was suffering from cirrhosis of the liver.

Meenaji came with us to the Moscow Film Festival in 1967 when *Teesri Kasam* was nominated in the best film category. Nargisji was a jury member for the children's film section and Sunil Dutt was there too. They asked the festival organizers to invite Meenaji, and I believe she had some medical treatment in Moscow.

NMK: Meena Kumari was extraordinary in *Sahib Bibi*. It was such a great film. Do you have a favourite Guru Dutt film?

WR: *Sahib Bibi* is very good and I like it very much. But my favourite is *Pyaasa*. It has such a smooth flow. The story of *Kaagaz Ke Phool* did not have a smooth flow.

NMK: *Pyaasa* and *Sahib Bibi* created a world that felt authentic— as a viewer you could almost imagine living among the people you were watching.

Now this might be an awkward question, but who actually directed *Sahib Bibi*? Was it Abrar Alvi or Guru Dutt? Is it something you can talk about?

WR: It's unfair to discuss it since Abrar is no more. I know Guruduttji did not always come on the sets. He would stay upstairs in his office at Natraj Studios. But he did come down to the set, if Abrar needed him.

When *Sahib Bibi* was being cast, I wanted to do Chhoti Bahu's role, but Meena Kumari had been cast. So I didn't think I would be part of the film. Then Abrar came over and told me he was going to direct it. It was news to me. He asked me to do Jabba's role. I was reminded of Guruduttji's advice not to play the secondary heroine. I was quite popular by then and so I refused. But Abrar insisted.

Guruduttji called me later and asked if I had agreed to do the film. He said: 'Rehman has the role of the Sahib, Meenaji is the Bibi and I play the Ghulam. Your role isn't the lead role.' I told him I agreed to play Jabba since I didn't want people to think I had refused because Abrar Alvi was directing the film.

On location in Panhala for Bees Saal Baad, *cast opposite Biswajit. The ghost story, a major hit, was released in the same year as* Sahib Bibi Aur Ghulam. *Circa 1962.*

I do recall telling Abrar Saab once that I didn't understand what he wanted me to do in some scene, and said he wasn't explaining it to me clearly. I did not complain to Guruduttji, but I think Murthy went and told him that I was finding it difficult.

NMK: What about the songs in the film? Who directed them?

WR: We shot the song 'Bhanwaraa badaa nadaan haye' and then the whole unit saw the rushes. Abrar Saab wasn't there that day.

I felt the shot taking was dull. So we told Guruduttji it was all right if he didn't want to direct the scenes, but he had to do the songs. He then spoke to Abrar and reshot the song brilliantly. He directed all the songs in *Sahib Bibi*.

NMK: I wonder why Guru Dutt decided not to sign any film as director after *Kaagaz Ke Phool*. Do you think it was because the film had flopped?

WR: It is very strange. He never told me he didn't want to direct any more. You mean he never directed again? What was his last film?

NMK: *Baharen Phir Bhi Aayengi*. Shahid Lateef directed it. The last film Guru Dutt signed was *Kaagaz Ke Phool*.

WR: Is it right for someone to get so disheartened by one flop? Everyone makes films that don't work.

His sister Lalli [the artist Lalitha Lajmi] told me once that Guruduttji suffered from depression. In the last years of his life he was very confused. We could all see that. He was unhappy. But no one realized just how depressed he was.

He started a film called *Raaz* in which I starred opposite Sunil Dutt. His chief assistant Niranjan was directing it. The story was something on the lines of *Woh Kaun Thi?*. Rehman Saab and I shot many good scenes, but Guruduttji shelved the film. When we asked why, he said: '*Nahin jam raha hai.*' [It isn't working.] Then he started *Gauri* with Geeta who wanted to act. He shelved that too.

NMK: Sadly none of the footage of the unfinished films exist. Maybe the failure of *Kaagaz Ke Phool* shook Guru Dutt's confidence and perhaps unnerved him.

WR: My husband suffered from depression as well and we didn't realize it. He started losing interest in everything. He didn't want to meet people and basically didn't feel like doing anything.

In the same way, no one knew how Guruduttji was really feeling. His brother Atmaram was not in India at the time. He was very fond of his sister Lalli, and very close to his mother, but I don't know whether he talked to them about his feelings.

NMK: There continues to be much speculation about your relationship with him. Everyone assumed that you were in love with each other. Did that cause a scandal when you were making films with him?

WR: Because his death was a mystery—no one knew for sure whether it was a suicide or an accident—there was much curiosity. His death was such a shock to us all. He was only thirty-nine. He was young. The question everyone asked was: 'Why did he have to die like that?'

None of my film colleagues have ever asked me personal questions about our relationship. It was always other people and the press who were curious, and still are, almost sixty years later.

I know we're public figures, but I strongly believe my private life should remain private. What ultimately matters and concerns the world is the work we leave behind.

NMK: Maybe it was because he filmed you in such a romantic and loving light that stirred this curiosity—which just doesn't seem to go away.

WR: It was true of the way he filmed others too. Don't you agree with me that Meena Kumari has never looked as beautiful as she did in *Sahib Bibi*?

You must know all directors want their leading lady to look special. I think a director has to be a little in love with his leading actress so he will project her as the most beautiful woman in the world. Considering the kind of romantic stories we make, this is a must.

Guruduttji was good to me and to many people, including Sadiq Saab and Johnny Walker, whom he introduced to films. In fact he was sensitive to everyone's needs. He helped me in many ways and guided my career. He was caring and protective. But in truth, he looked out for everyone.

NMK: Do you remember when you worked with Guru Dutt for the last time?

WR: It must have been in 1961 or 1962. I don't remember the exact date—but it was during the filming of the final scene in *Sahib Bibi*. Jabba is waiting for Bhoothnath in a carriage in the haveli ruins. That was the last time we worked together. He never offered me another role after *Sahib Bibi*.

I was in Madras when Guruduttji passed away. I had gone there for a charity cricket match with a group of stars. Dilip Saab was there too. The actress Shammi Rabadi, who is a close friend of mine, came and told me she had some very bad news. She said: 'Guru Dutt is no more.' Oh my God, I was completely stunned. I knew he had tried to commit suicide before, but it was still a terrible shock. I immediately flew back to Bombay. This was on 10 October 1964. There were many people at the funeral, including Raj Kapoor and Dev Anand. It was a very sad day.

NMK: Do you recall when you last saw him? Or spoke to him?

WR: Abrar, my sister Sayeeda and I had gone to the Berlin Film Festival in June 1963 where *Sahib Bibi* was screened. Guruduttji joined us there. No one liked the film in Berlin. They found it slow, despite the fact that a shorter version was screened there on the evening of 27 June. The festival director asked me: 'If Chhoti Bahu is so unhappy with her husband, why doesn't she go away with Bhoothnath?' *[laughs]* I said: 'It doesn't happen like that in our culture.'

Their culture is totally different. I tried explaining why the aristocrats of that time could do no such thing. In fact, when

Chhoti Bahu steps out of the house for the first time, she is murdered for having broken with tradition. Besides, Chhoti Bahu is not in love with Bhoothnath and neither does he love her—it is her sadness and beauty that fascinate him.

Guruduttji was present at the screening, but he left Berlin the following day.

NMK: The Berlin Film Festival was held between 21 June and 2 July 1963. So that means you did not meet him for over a year, and then you heard he had passed away in October 1964. Is that right?

WR: Yes. The last time I saw him must have been in Berlin. We did not work together after *Sahib Bibi*.

Losing someone is always upsetting. Even though Yash Chopra was eighty his death was a shock to me. I met Yashji at Amitabh Bachchan's seventieth birthday party about ten days before Yashji passed away. He hugged me and said he was feeling tired and wanted to go home. His wife, Pamela, thought they should stay at the party a little longer. I think Yashji was admitted to the hospital a few days later. The next thing I heard was that he had passed away. I was very sad.

So you can imagine what a shock Guruduttji's death was for his family, for me and for all the people who worked closely with him.

We must, however, think of the amazing respect he has in the world today. No other Indian director after Satyajit Ray has, I believe, that kind of international recognition and admiration.

NMK: That is true. It is ironic that Guru Dutt's fame spread after his death—something he predicted in *Pyaasa* as being the fate of some artists. But few Indian film-makers have as enduring a power as he has.

I also believe if popular Indian cinema had been better known in the West in the 1950s, Guru Dutt would have most certainly been counted among world cinema's finest directors. He had such a singular voice and vision.

WR: I am lucky to have worked in his films. I don't believe they will ever be forgotten.

NMK: You have contributed to many classics and I can imagine it is satisfying to have such a substantial legacy. I am not sure how many Indian actors will leave behind as many memorable films. I'd like to ask you about another important film in your career—*Mujhe Jeene Do*. Set in the Chambal Valley of Madhya Pradesh, this tale about a dacoit and a dancer was among the highest-earning films in 1963.

What made Sunil Dutt decide to produce a dacoit story?

WR: From the early 1960s, Vinoba Bhave and Jayaprakash Narayan encouraged the Chambal River Valley dacoits to surrender. It was around the same time that the story of dacoits became a popular subject in Hindi cinema. The trend started in

1960 with Raj Kapoor's *Jis Desh Mein Ganga Behti Hai*. In 1961 came *Gunga Jumna* with Dilip Saab and in 1963 Sunil Dutt released *Mujhe Jeene Do*, directed by Moni Bhattacharjee who had worked as Bimal Roy's assistant on the classic films *Do Bigha Zamin* and *Madhumati*.

You could say even *Sholay* was about a dacoit, Gabbar Singh. And Sunil Dutt himself had played a good son turned dacoit in *Mother India*. When we were shooting *Mujhe Jeene Do*, Sunilji told me about an incident that took place during the making of *Mother India*. He had to play an emotional scene and, to get the emotion right, Mehboob Saab asked him to lie face down on the ground. He then stood on Sunilji's back and twisted his arm. When he screamed in pain, Mehboob Saab said: 'I want you to cry out just like that in the shot!' I told Sunilji I hoped he had no intention of doing that to me. *[we laugh]*

NMK: I read an article by Deepak Mahan [*The Hindu*, 13 May 2010] in which he interviewed several former outlaws who believed *Mujhe Jeene Do* had the most authentic depiction of dacoit life while they felt that films like *Sholay* were glamorized figments of imagination that bore no connection to reality.

WR: Sunil Dutt's intention was to show the reality of dacoits, and that was the interesting thing about the film—eighty-five per cent of the story was based on real-life incidents, including those involving the notorious 'daaku' Maan Singh.

We had police protection while we were shooting the film

A day off during the filming of Sunil Dutt's Mujhe Jeene Do. *Chambal Valley, circa 1962.*

in the ravines of Bhind–Morena. I remember hearing about a woman who had been kidnapped and who later became a dacoit. One of her hands had been cut off and so she had to fire her gun with one hand. I have forgotten her name, but it is a true story. Her daughter came to see me during the filming of *Mujhe Jeene Do* and, when she saw our costumes, she said: 'My mother never wore a *ghagra-choli*, she wore pants.'

NMK: So much for the costume department!

You play the prostitute Chamelijaan in the film. She is a woman who is abducted by the dacoit Jarnail Singh [Sunil Dutt] who falls in love with her when he sees her dancing at a wedding. What kind of person is Chameli?

WR: She has a defiant nature and although she is at Jarnail Singh's mercy, she refuses to dance for him and tells him: 'I dance at happy occasions—at weddings or when children are born. But your hands are stained with blood. Because of you, women become widows and children are orphaned. What right do you have to tell me to dance?' I thought that was a good scene.

Portraying Chamelijaan was a challenge because her character goes through many transformations—from dancing girl to wife, wife to protective mother—I needed to express a range of emotions.

A character touches me if I believe the events in the film could actually happen to someone in real life. Then I can perform better. When the characters and storylines are too unreal, my work isn't very good. My heart isn't in it. But great actors like Dilip Saab, Amitabh or Naseeruddin Shah can perform well even when the character, or the dramatic situations they need to bring alive, seem artificial. I can't do that.

NMK: *Mujhe Jeene Do* has your exquisite song 'Raat bhi hai kuch bheegi bheegi' by Jaidev and Sahir. You perform the dance in the wedding scene where Jarnail Singh and his band of dacoits see you for the first time.

WR: I liked that song very much. Lachhu Maharaj choreographed it so beautifully. His mudras and bhavas were very delicate. The facial expressions were soft and Lata Mangeshkar sang the song with such sensitivity that she made it easy for me to convey the right tone and mood.

The dance itself was not difficult. However, the way it was filmed was technically complicated. I danced on a large mirror that had been painted black, but the mirror reflected everything and so lighting the set was tricky. The end result, however, created a mysterious and interesting effect.

NMK: Have you noticed how often Hindi films, particularly the older ones, have a song performed for an audience within the story? The heroine is dancing and the hero sits among the onlookers. Or the hero is singing and the heroine, looking embarrassed and awkward, is a guest at a party. We could call it a performance within a performance.

I have always wondered if the popularity of this setting is a harking back to cinema's theatre origins by recreating a performance and an audience.

WR: I have no idea why this kind of setting became popular. There are many examples—the hero plays the piano and sings a sad song. Or the heroine is dancing while the hero mingles among the party guests and watches her dance.

I know that distributors used to worry if a film only had five songs, and so film-makers would be more or less obliged to add a few more songs. Perhaps the party scene was an easy scene to add.

NMK: I suppose it could fit into any story and so we see it in all sorts of films.

You have worked in the black-and-white and the colour film eras. Did the switch affect the way you worked?

WR: When we started shooting colour films—and I was told this later—the film speed, the emulsion's sensitivity to light, was not very high. As a result, they needed hard lights and reflectors, and these were very harsh on our skin and eyes. It was uncomfortable for us actors.

When colour-film speed increased, the lighting became softer. That helped a lot.

NMK: Is it true that black-and-white photography required you to wear colours like yellow or red to enhance the contrast?

WR: Yes, it is true. Strong and dark colours helped to increase the contrast and we were particularly asked not to wear pure white in black-and-white films. They said it reflected light. We mostly wore pastel blues, off-whites and pale greens.

NMK: Colour photography took over Indian cinema very late, as compared to Hollywood. So you have both black-and-white and colour films being produced side by side till the late 1960s. When colour photography did take over, one can honestly say the films were not sophisticatedly lit through the 1970s and '80s. The lighting wasn't very good, the zoom lens didn't help and even the make-up, especially for male actors, exaggerated the problem. Faces were powdered white while you could see the hands and neck of the actor were his natural colour.

I remember visiting a film set in the early 1980s and hearing the camera assistant cry out: 'Full light!' And all the lights went on and every inch of the set was lit with the same intensity. No shading, no pools of darkness to create atmosphere.

WR: You're right. It took time for Indian films to be photographed properly in colour. For colour to work well, the lighting has to be subdued and soft. In the early days they wanted to show as many colours as possible—everything had to been bold and brash. It was to show they were making a film in colour rather than making the story work. *[we laugh]*

Many years after I had more or less stopped working, I returned to the sets for Karan Johar's *Kabhi Khushi Kabhie Gham*. When I saw the set, I wondered where all the lights had gone because the lighting was so soft. I was told they now use reflected light.

I don't know if you know this, but I was supposed to play Amitabh's mother in Karan's film. I shot for a day, but on that same day my husband fell very ill and had to be admitted to hospital. So I pulled out of *K3G*.

NMK: I didn't realize you were cast in the film. That would have been interesting.

Coming back to film photography, *K3G* and most Indian movies are now beautifully shot in colour. But I think it's a real shame that young audiences are just not attracted to black-and-white films any more. They're happy to see old song clips on television, but would they go to the cinema to see an old classic on the big screen? This is more or less true of young audiences around the world.

I am sure you will agree with me that the black-and-white film has a more textured and cinematic mood. It also evokes nostalgia and the past.

WR: Things have to change. I like films in colour, but I agree black-and-white films had a more textured atmosphere. Dramatic moments could also be brought out in a far more interesting way.

That said, Dwarka Divecha who photographed *Dil Diya Dard Liya*, and Fali Mistry who shot *Guide* did a great job despite the technical limitations of their era. I was lucky to have worked with them and other gifted cinematographers like V.K. Murthy, Jal Mistry, Faredoon A. Irani and Subrata Mitra in *Teesri Kasam*. They were all excellent and worked well in black and white and colour.

NMK: It is clear that you are very aware of how films are made. Have you ever considered directing?

WR: I had an offer from the Barjatyas once. Some time ago they were planning to ask artists of our generation to direct a film. I said no because I thought it would be hard work. It wasn't that I was scared of hard work—I still am not. But perhaps I wasn't confident of doing justice to a film.

I did start to have a better understanding of film-making once I had made my third or fourth film—I knew about frame compositions, camera movements and angles, the different kinds of shots, etc. But all this took time to understand. I think I have a good story sense, and can make constructive suggestions. I know more or less what works and how to make some scenes better. My problem is that I am too logical and Hindi cinema does not bother much about logic.

I remember asking my film directors: 'How is this scene possible? How can this character do this?' I always got the same answer: 'We have to exaggerate and elaborate. If we

On the sets of Guide. *Circa 1964.*

stick to logic, the film won't be interesting and it will not run.'

NMK: It would be fascinating to see a film directed by you. I have always wondered if actors make good directors because they know the difficulties of performing a scene—how to make it work.

What would a director say to you that was the most helpful when approaching a scene?

WR: I wanted the directors to explain things clearly. I could grasp things very quickly and worked by instinct. But my weak point was my voice. My voice modulation was not very good.

Some directors said I spoke my lines too quickly. They would ask me to talk slower and pause at certain points. Otherwise I don't think they needed to instruct me in detail.

An actor's voice is very important, especially on the stage, where you must have the ability to throw your voice well. In films you can convey mood—angry, happy or shy—through silent expressions. I am not saying film acting is only about silent expressions because dialogue delivery is important too. But I was well aware I didn't have a beautiful voice like Meena Kumari or Dilip Saab. They were great actors with great voices and diction.

NMK: Were you ever tempted to act on the stage?

WR: I was very keen. Shashi Kapoor used to run Prithvi Theatre, and I asked him if we could do a play together. He thought it was a good idea, but he was extremely busy. People forget just how popular he was. He made several films at the same time and worked two or three shifts a day—going from one set to another, from one film to another.

In later years, Girish Karnad and Arundhati Nag and others asked me to act in their plays. Now I think what if I am on the stage and forget my lines? Why make a fool of myself?

NMK: When I interviewed Gulzar Saab he said, unlike stage acting, the difficulty for film actors is expressing themselves in bursts of performance. You do a shot, sit down and sometime later you do the next shot. It's an off-and-on kind of performance.

WR: That is difficult. Plus, when you go back in front of the camera after a break—which could be a long or a short break—you have to match the mood, the intensity and the momentum of your last take.

When I had a difficult scene to do, I'd ask my director to film the whole scene in a master shot, so the emotions would come out in a single flow. Later the scene could be divided into close-ups and wide shots, or whatever.

This was helpful because it allowed us actors to perform the scene from start to finish. Otherwise if we did a shot, sat down, had tea and then went back in front of the camera—the continuity of mood and emotion was gone.

NMK: I hear that Naseeruddin Shah prefers doing a scene in a master shot too. It takes a skilled actor to hold the shot for a long time, especially without having many retakes.

I was surprised when Guruswamy told me in an interview years ago that Guru Dutt would ask for many retakes.

WR: Everyone thought the retakes in *Pyaasa* were needed because of me, given that I was the newcomer. To the contrary! It was Guruduttji who had this habit of asking for take after take. Sometimes he was not sure what he wanted from a scene. But when you keep retaking the same shot, your performance becomes stale and mechanical. Your dialogue delivery can end up sounding flat and lifeless.

I remember Guruswamy once called me at home—I was not needed on the set as Guruduttji and Mala Sinha were shooting a long dialogue scene that takes place in Mr Ghosh's office—and he said: 'Come now! You must see what's going on. You get worried about retakes—come and watch these veterans. They started the shot yesterday and are still at it.' *[we laugh]*

NMK: Even recently, V.K. Murthy in an interview referred to the scene you just spoke about and said that Guru Dutt asked for 104 takes! Clearly he was not easily satisfied with his acting. So how did he judge his own performance?

WR: He would ask his chief assistant or Abrar if his take was okay. Murthy sometimes told him if he thought Guruduttji could do the shot better.

NMK: Did you need many retakes?

WR: My first take was usually good, the second was less good and by the third take my energy level completely dropped. Even if the first take was fine, the directors would invariably say: 'One more. For safety.' If you asked the director why—was there something lacking in the performance? What went wrong?—no one would give me a clear answer.

The only directors who explained the need for a retake

With brother-in-law Abdul Malik (elder sister Shahida's husband) at Vauhini Studios, Madras, during the making of Rakhi. *Circa 1962.*

were Guruduttji, Satyajit Ray, Asit Sen, Vijay Anand, Basu Bhattacharya and A. Subba Rao, the man who made *Milan.* I made *Darpan* with him in 1970. These directors explained things clearly to me: 'Your pitch was too high. Modulate your voice like this.' Or whatever. But most directors never said anything.

NMK: Some directors do not like showing the actor the rushes—or dailies, as they are also called. During the 1950s, you mentioned the cast and crew saw the rushes and trial shows. Were actors always encouraged to do this?

WR: Yes. And for many years the whole unit would watch the songs too.

After the screening, the director would decide if he needed to retake a shot or a scene, to improve it. Sometimes the microphone boom had dropped into the frame—if it wasn't very obvious, and just at the edge of the frame, the director would let it pass, but if it had dropped too low into the shot, we were obliged to redo the shot. Sometimes there were problems with unwanted shadows.

If a performance really did not work because the dialogue delivery was not up to the mark, or the emotions were not coming through, the director would film a close-up and insert it into the scene to enhance the drama. We didn't necessarily refilm the whole scene because the set might have been destroyed by then. A close-up is easy to insert. This process is what we called 'patch work'.

At the start of the multi-starrer era, the 1970s directors, including Yash Chopra, stopped showing us the rushes because many top stars would create a fuss: 'Oh, my scene was cut? Why is that?' Or they would say: 'I think we should retake the shot.' They thought they could improve on their performance, even if the director did not think it was necessary.

As far as I was concerned, I told all my directors I wanted to see the final film and did not mind if any of my scenes were edited out.

NMK: For some decades now, actors and directors have been able to judge a performance on set thanks to the video assist [a device which allows a viewing of a video version of the take immediately after it is filmed]. In your time there was no possibility of watching the take until you saw the rushes the next day.

WR: I never liked the idea of looking at the video monitor. I trusted the director. Even when I thought I had given a good shot, I waited for his reaction.

I remember Dilip Saab sometimes commenting on my performance when we were doing a scene together. He would say: 'Waheeda, you speak too fast. Say your lines a little slower, take a pause.'

NMK: But it sounds like you never feared the camera.

WR: No, I didn't really because I had made Telugu and Tamil films before working in Hindi cinema. Don't forget I was used to dancing on the stage before joining films, so the fear and nervousness had long gone.

NMK: In the early 1960s, soon after the release of *Kaagaz Ke Phool*, you were offered a part in *Abhijan*, which was released in 1962. The film was based on Tarashankar Bandopadhyay's popular novel.

How did Satyajit Ray approach you?

WR: The editor of *Filmfare*, B.K. Karanjia, sent someone to my house with a letter from Mr Ray that said: 'My leading man Soumitra Chatterjee and my unit believe that you are most suitable for the role of Gulaabi, the heroine of my next film. If you agree to play the part, we'll be very pleased.' I was very happy and could not believe Satyajit Ray had thought of me.

A few days later I called Mr Ray in Calcutta and the first thing he said was: 'Waheeda, you earn a lot of money in Hindi films. I make films on small budgets.'

'Saab, why are you embarrassing me? It is an honour for me. You have shown me much respect by asking me to work with

(L to R) Sunil Dutt, Satyajit Ray and Nargis at the 1973 Berlin Film Festival where Reshma Aur Shera *and* Ashani Sanket *were screened. Photograph: Waheeda Rehman.*

you. There is no problem about the money. I prefer you don't mention it.'

I explained to him that I didn't speak Bengali, and he said the character he wanted me to play, Gulaabi, is from the Bihar–Bengal border and talks in a mix of Bhojpuri and Bengali. Therefore the language should not be a problem for me. He also added: 'Remember you can't come to shoot for four days and then go back to Bombay. We have to film in one stretch, from start to finish.' I agreed and assured him I'd work out my dates with my Bombay producers.

Soon after our call, I went to Calcutta and met Mr Ray. He gave me an audio tape of my dialogue to make it easier for me to memorize my lines.

NMK: What was your first impression of him?

WR: He had such a towering personality. He had a deep voice and a particular style of speaking.

I was a little nervous at the beginning of the shoot because I was working in an unfamiliar language and, after all, he was a world-famous director with such a huge reputation. But Mr Ray was reassuring and said: 'I have more confidence in you than you have in yourself. You'll live up to my expectations.' I think it was his way of making me feel at ease.

Ray Saab was meticulous and explained everything in great detail. He sketched every scene and made detailed shot breakdowns, even noting the lens he planned to use. His storyboarding was extremely helpful. In those days no one had heard of storyboarding. He was also one of the few directors who gave me a bound script.

There was a scene in *Abhijan* where I am sitting in a *ghoda gaadi* [horse carriage] and a sethji is forcibly taking me away. Soumitra [Chatterjee] comes, I look at him and jump out of the carriage and run away. Before Ray Saab could say anything to me, I glanced at the sethji and jumped out. Mr Ray quickly said: 'I was about to ask you to do just that. But you did it before I could say anything!'

NMK: Do you remember how many months the filming took?

WR: Months? I think the shooting was over in nineteen days. Soumitra had many more scenes than I did and perhaps had to work for a further week or so.

I remember a short scene in which I had to speak some lines, sing and do a little dance—not the Bharatanatyam or a filmy dance—just move my hands as I was talking to the hero. I asked if a song had been recorded for me and Mr Ray said: 'No, you will sing.'

'But I don't know how to sing, and my voice isn't good.'

He said: 'We're used to the voices of Lata Mangeshkar and Asha Bhonsle, but I want to hear Waheeda's voice. Gulaabi is a simple village girl, and if her voice isn't perfect, it will sound natural. That's the effect I want. You're forgetting that my films are realistic.'

He told me the entire scene would be filmed in one shot. 'Come to the studio. Rehearse for a day and then we'll shoot. You're a dancer. Why are you getting nervous?'

'Ray Saab, the dance is not difficult, but I also have to say my lines and convey the emotions—she is sad, she laughs and sings too.' Soumitra was most reassuring and told me not to worry.

We rehearsed for about four to five hours in the morning and after lunch we finished the scene in two takes.

Satyajit Ray made films the way films should be made—from start to finish. So whether you're needed on the set or not, you can spend your whole time thinking about your character. It's not just about learning the dialogue and facing the camera, you must somewhat live the role and not always be acting it.

NMK: Did you ever discuss the possibility of Mr Ray making a film in Hindi?

WR: His wife would ask me to encourage him to do so. When I spoke to him about it, he said: 'Some day I want to, but then you have all those lengthy songs and dances and all that.'

'No, make it according to your style.'

I think he was reluctant to make a film in Hindi because he did not know Hindi well and believed that was essential. 'The most important thing is having command over the language. So I can tell if the actor's tone is not right. One thing is certain—if I make a Hindi movie, I will cast you.'

NMK: Why do you think Mrs Ray wanted her husband to make a Hindi movie?

WR: Regional films have a smaller reach while Hindi cinema is shown all over India. Perhaps Mrs Ray wanted more people to see his work. His films did well in Bengal, and were occasionally screened in other cities, and people abroad loved them. When he became an important figure in world cinema, then the whole of India started paying more attention to him. But his films were not widely distributed here.

Many years later when he was making *Shatranj Ke Khilari*, he called me and said: 'Waheeda, I promised to cast you, but I don't feel the role in this film will suit you.'

I think the last time I saw him was when he came to Bombay for the dubbing of *Shatranj Ke Khilari*. He called and said he wanted to come over. He dropped by and we talked for a while.

NMK: I had the pleasure of looking after him during his week-long stay in Paris in 1983, and then met him later in Calcutta. He had a formidable personality and made such extraordinary films. They get better as the years go by.

You say you were lucky to have worked with Satyajit Ray, Guru Dutt, Vijay Anand, Raj Khosla and others. These are precisely the directors who would expect a lot from their actors.

But what kind of roles attracted you?

WR: I wanted to do different kinds of films, and if I was offered the same type of role I refused. It did not excite me to do the same thing over and over again. There is no challenge in repeating oneself because one tends to perform mechanically.

In the 1960s, most Hindi films were light romances. Boy falls in love with girl. Some obstacle comes in their way, usually created by the parents or a villain, or there is a difference of class between them—the boy is poor and the girl is rich—and ultimately the boy wins the girl.

NMK: I was talking to the director Kalpana Lajmi about your work and she said you always showed a willingness to take chances by choosing atypical roles.

WR: I tried. Some of the films I acted in were not the typical sort. Think of *Pyaasa*, *Mujhe Jeene Do*, *Khamoshi*, *Guide* or *Reshma Aur Shera*.

NMK: Another unusual film you made was *Teesri Kasam*, which was based on a story called 'Maare Gaye Gulfaam' by the celebrated Hindi writer Renu. That was the second time you were cast opposite Raj Kapoor after *Ek Dil Sao Afsane* in 1963.

WR: When I heard Rajji was going to play Hiraman, the hero of the film, a bullock-cart driver, I wondered how he would look in a dhoti. Sometimes you have a strong image of someone and you can't imagine that person as another personality. I had seen *Awara* and many Raj Kapoor movies. He was very influenced

101

With (L to R) sister Zahida, Nargis, Amitabh Bachchan, Sunil Dutt, Vinod Khanna, Amrish Puri and Sukhdev during the Reshma Aur Shera *shoot. Rajasthan, 1971.*

by Charlie Chaplin and imitated him. Rajji had sad eyes.

It turned out that Raj Kapoor was excellent as Hiraman. He had no mannerisms and acted in a natural style. Actually, we were both encouraged not to *act* in the true sense of the word. The Bengali director Basu Bhattacharya wanted us to perform in a natural style, to give a lifelike performance. Most Bengali directors asked their actors to be natural. They also preferred filming away from the studio on real locations to enhance a sense of realism in their stories. So some scenes of *Teesri Kasam* were filmed near the Powai Lake, and the rest was shot in Bina, a small town near Bhopal.

Rajji thought the ending of the film should be changed and Hiraman and Hirabai should go away together. But no one agreed to that. The whole point of the story was Hiraman's '*teesri kasam*' [third vow]—never to let a *nautanki* girl travel in his cart again. The writer Renu—who had also written the dialogue for the film—would have been furious if the ending had been changed.

I must tell you about an extraordinary incident that happened at the end of the *Teesri Kasam* shoot. We had to travel to Bina by train, as there were no flights in those days. When the shooting was over, Rajji, two of his friends, my sister Sayeeda, my hairdresser and I made our way to the station to leave on an early afternoon train for Bombay.

We got on to the train and settled in our air-conditioned compartments. We heard the train engine start and then stop. We assumed it must be some technical problem because again the train started and stopped. Finally, we looked out of the compartment window to see what was going on. The railway station at Bina was very small and on either side of the train we could see huge crowds of students on the platforms. Then we heard people shouting: '*Utro, utro, dekhna hai, dekhna hai.*' [Get down! We want to see you.]

Someone came and asked Rajji to talk to the student leaders and tell them to calm the crowd down. Rajji opened the door and talked to a group of young men who had gathered near the compartment door. They told him that the local students had wanted to watch the shooting of *Teesri Kasam*, but were

Receiving the Silver Medal award for Teesri Kasam *from President Radhakrishnan in Delhi. 1966.*

repeatedly given the wrong location address by the production team. By the time they cycled to the spot, having bunked their classes, they could not find a soul there. Apparently, this had happened over many days and so they did not get the chance to see Rajji and me. Now they were very insistent about seeing us.

But Rajji immediately said: 'You have seen me, but Waheeda Rehman is not coming out.'

'Why not? We're her fans.'

He was adamant: 'No, she won't come out. She is a woman.' Rajji's reply incited them further and they said: 'So what? She must see her fans or else we will not allow the train to leave the station.'

The situation became very tense. I don't know what came over Rajji but he dug his heels in and said: 'No!' Then he closed the compartment door. That did it! The crowd became furious and started hurling stones and hitting the train with big iron bars. They did not let the train move an inch. We had to duck down in our compartments to avoid being hurt while Rajji was getting more and more enraged. He wanted to go out and confront the crowd. His friends tried to restrain him and, when they realized they couldn't, they pushed him into our compartment and said: 'Ladies! Take care of him. He has gone wild.'

And so the three of us—Sayeeda, my hairdresser and I—had to literally pin Rajji on to the seat. I sat on his chest while my sister held on to his legs. He became red as a tomato and tried to wriggle out of our grip while we were struggling to keep him down. We kept imploring him: 'No, Rajji, no!' To which he protested: 'Let me go! Let me go!' *[we laugh]*

It became such a drama—but maybe I should say a comedy! In the meantime, our angry fans had wrecked the train. There was shouting and pelting. Finally the police arrived and dispersed the crowd. We somehow got to Bhopal in the early evening and had to wait for hours while the police report and the railway department report were written up.

The next day we arrived at Bombay Central. The people who came to receive us were shocked to see the terrible state we were in. We had fragments of glass lodged in our hair and sprayed on our clothes—we even found bits of glass in our bags.

NMK: It sounds really scary and dangerous.

WR: It *was* very dangerous. These are also some of the things we go through. Our lives are not always a bed of roses as many people assume.

NMK: But I wonder why Raj Kapoor had such a reaction.

WR: It was strange. I tried to tell him I could stand behind him at the compartment door and so the fans would see me. But he said: 'No! I have told them no. Why should they look at a woman anyway?'

I said: 'What do you mean? I am a woman, but I am seen in the movies. That's my work. Why can't they see me?'

'No! They won't see my heroine.' He could not be persuaded otherwise. *[laughs]*

NMK: I suppose when you're famous and filming in small towns where people didn't have access to stars, especially in the 1960s, this situation is unsurprising.

You have worked with a number of former Bimal Roy assistants, including Basu Bhattacharya, Moni Bhattarcharjee and Gulzar. How did you meet the *Teesri Kasam* director?

WR: In the early 1960s, Shailendra, who produced the film, called to say he wanted to come over to discuss a film and brought Basuda to the house. It was Basuda's first film. They offered me the role of Hirabai and I said no. I had this bad habit of saying no at first. Why? I don't know. Shailendra said I should sleep over it and then decide. This is what all the producers would say. When he called again, I lied to him saying Guruduttji was starting a movie and I was working in it.

But then Shailendra called Guruduttji who said: '*Hein?* What movie?' Immediately Guruduttji called me: 'Did you say no to Shailendra? Why? Don't you want to earn money to run the house? If you sit at home, how will you manage? And another thing. Why did you lie?'

'I didn't know what to do. I lied.'

'That isn't good. Shailendra is a very nice person. You must do it. I can't understand you. This is bad. I think you're a lazy person.' *[laughs]*

Teesri Kasam took a long time in production and was finally released in 1966.

NMK: It was the only film that Shailendra produced and I believe he had a lot of financial problems completing the film.

WR: He had to really struggle hard. One day he came to see me and said he couldn't pay me. I felt very bad for him. He had tears in his eyes. It is heartbreaking to see a man cry. I told him not to talk about the money.

Shailendra wrote beautiful songs for the film. I loved 'Sajan re jhoot mat bolo.'

NMK: Your era had the best songs.

You must have met a number of composers over the years, but did you also get to know any of the lyricists?

WR: Sometimes Majrooh Saab visited my sets. He once sent me kebabs when we were in Panchgani on a location shoot.

Once I had to go to Madh Island for the shoot of *Girl Friend*. My car broke down and so I took a cab. When I got there the director was upset with me and said I should not have risked travelling all that way alone in a taxi. I told him I didn't want the shoot to get delayed.

I don't know how but Majrooh Saab heard about this incident, and when we met a few days later, he said: 'Bibi, never do that again. Damn the shoot! Do you realize what a desolate and lonely place Madh Island is? And you went there alone in a taxi? Don't show so much dedication! Next time, phone me and I'll send you my car.'

And of course I met Shailendra many times during the making of *Teesri Kasam.*

NMK: I once interviewed Dev Anand about how he chose Shailendra for *Guide* rather than Sahir Ludhianvi, who was the Navketan favourite. Dev Saab said he happened to meet Shailendra on a flight and he expressed his desire to work on *Guide*. Dev Saab readily agreed because apparently Sahir and S.D. Burman were not getting on well at that time. Shailendra's songs were indeed superb in *Guide*, this key film in your career.

Visiting Dev Anand on the sets of Prem Pujari. *Circa 1969. Waheeda Rehman made the maximum number of films (seven) opposite Dev Anand.*

Were you familiar with R.K. Narayan's novel before starting the film?

WR: It was Mr Ray who asked me to read the novel because he was considering adapting it. He told me if the film ever took off, he would cast me as Rosie. She had to be a good dancer and he knew south Indians were usually good dancers, and so he had thought of me.

I had forgotten all about it when a year or two later Dev told me he was producing the film. I asked: 'You mean R.K. Narayan's novel? But isn't Mr Ray making it?'

Dev said: 'No, no, I know about that. I have bought the rights of the book.'

Satyajit Ray would have conceived the film in a completely different way. But I believe I was fated to play Rosie, no matter who was going to direct the film. Many actresses were keen to play Rosie, including Padmini and Leela Naidu. They sent me letters saying I should let them know if for any reason I did not accept the part.

NMK: I never knew Mr Ray wanted to make a film based on R.K. Narayan's novel. That will be a surprise to many. Yet he clearly thought the role of Rosie was perfect for you, just as no one but Nargis could have played Radha in *Mother India*.

WR: Or Meena Kumari as Chhoti Bahu in *Sahib Bibi Aur Ghulam.*

NMK: Absolutely right.

You seemed to suggest there was a possibility that you might not have played Rosie. Is that right?

WR: I almost didn't, because Dev announced that Raj Khosla was going to direct. I said: 'Dev, have you forgotten how we quarrelled during the making of *Solva Saal*?'

'Forget it, my friend. Everyone fights in life. Come on now, *Guide* is a very big picture, Waheeda. It is going to be made in English and in Hindi. Don't be like that. You are a mature person and Raj has changed.'

I don't know what happened but in the end Dev decided against Raj Khosla as director.

NMK: What was your disagreement with Raj Khosla? Was this during the making of *Solva Saal*?

WR: That's right. You see in the film I play a naive sixteen-year-old girl who is in love with a boy who promises to marry her. We elope and foolishly I take all my dead mother's jewellery with me. We catch a train and, halfway through the journey, the boy steals the jewellery and disappears. I am distraught and decide to commit suicide. I get off the train and head towards the sea. Dev, a co-passenger, has been watching me all the while and has understood the whole situation. He follows me and saves me from drowning.

Our clothes are wet, and so we go to a nearby dhobi ghat

and the dhobi lends us some clothes till our clothes have dried. What do I see? The costume department gives me a chiffon sari and a strapless blouse. I looked at Raj Khosla and asked: 'Rajji, am I going to wear this?'

He said: 'I know you! Try it, but if you don't feel comfortable, wear whatever you want.'

So I went to my make-up room where my mother was sitting. I put on the sari and the strapless blouse and looked at myself in the mirror. 'I can't wear this.' I took the blouse off and put on another blouse with sleeves. When I returned to the set, Raj Khosla saw me and lost his cool. 'You don't listen to your director. Who do you think you are? Madhubala? Meena Kumari? Nargis? Only two of your pictures have been released, and you want to have your way.'

He reminded me how I had insisted on keeping my name when I first signed the contract with Guru Dutt Films, and the fuss I made about the costumes in *C.I.D.* But I said: 'Rajji, you told me if I didn't feel comfortable, I didn't have to wear this blouse. It didn't feel right.' Dev then turned to me and asked: 'Waheeda, what's the problem? What difference does it make?'

I explained to Dev: 'In this scene the hero asks me my name and I say it is Laajwanti [bashful/shy]. And he says: *"Tabhi toh itni laaj aati hai."'* [That's why you're so shy.]

If this is the dialogue in the scene, I asked Raj Khosla, would this shy sixteen-year-old wear revealing clothes in front of a man who is an utter stranger at that point of the story? He said: 'Oh, now you are talking about logic. Is this your counterargument?'

'I think it would be amusing if we were given baggy, ill-fitting clothes and looked like clowns. That would create a moment of comedy.'

'*Lo ji*, now she's telling me how to direct.'

Raj Khosla decided to wrap for the day. The next day we returned to the set. Everyone had calmed down. I wore a different blouse and we carried on shooting.

NMK: You had a point. If the girl is called Laajwanti, her name assumes an innocent sort of character and revealing clothes would have been inappropriate.

I must say I really liked *Solva Saal*. It is a charming film and Raj Khosla directed it beautifully. Interestingly, there isn't a hint of tension in your performance.

Did you ever work with him again?

WR: After my two children were born, Amarjeet, Dev's good friend who made *Hum Dono*, was producing a picture called *Sunny*. He was going to introduce Sunny Deol in it and offered me the role of the mother. I agreed and then Amarjeet quickly added: 'Now you're married and have children. Time has passed. I have to tell you—Raj Khosla is the director.'

When I told my husband, Shashi, about the offer, he said: 'Come on, grow up now. It doesn't matter if you argued in the past. Do it. It isn't right to say no.' I said yes to Amarjeet and played the mother's role in *Sunny*.

Raj Khosla was a very good director. He filmed songs very

well. We had our arguments, but he was a very nice person to spend time with. He was a cheerful fellow. Guruduttji was quiet and Raj Khosla was the lively one. In later years, when we both became more mature, we put all our differences behind us.

NMK: Coming back to *Guide*, what happened after Raj Khosla was dropped from the project?

WR: Chetan Anand started work on the Hindi *Guide*, and the English version was the American director Tad Danielewski's responsibility. At first neither of them wanted me as Rosie. By that time, I wasn't sure I wanted to do the film either. But Guruduttji sent word through Murthy that I must do it.

When the shooting began there was a clash between Tad and Chetan Saab almost immediately. They both wanted different camera positions, and the lighting took hours.

NMK: Do you mean to say you filmed a scene in Hindi and then shot the same scene in English?

WR: That's right. They needed to save money. Both language versions had the same sets and the same locations. That's how we worked. But it wasn't happening. Tad and Chetan Saab had their egos.

It wasn't long before Dev came to my make-up room and said: 'Waheeda, see how much time they're taking. One says put the camera here, the other says put it over there. Tad wants one action and Chetan Saab another. And their endless discussions! I think we should first finish the English version then think about the Hindi *Guide*.'

That's what happened. We first completed the English *Guide* and when it came to the Hindi *Guide*, Dev asked Goldie [Vijay Anand] to take over. I knew Goldie from the *Kala Bazar* days. He wrote excellent dialogue.

NMK: How did you like working with Tad Danielewski? He was the only American director you worked with.

WR: Tad was very vague. Whenever I asked him anything, he would say: 'Maybe, maybe.'

You can say that sometimes, but not all the time. You need the director to be clear. Should Rosie react warmly? Or should she react coldly?

NMK: You mean the director has to be decisive and bring out shades of the character's behaviour?

WR: Yes. Saying 'maybe' doesn't help. Goldie would explain precisely how the scene should be played. You can get angry or upset with a director, but he must be clear. Satyajit Ray was very clear—it was either yes or no.

Acting is an understanding between actor and director. Performance comes from that combination of minds. I may act

With Kishore Sahu and Tad Danielewski, the American director of the
English Guide, *on location at the Elephanta Caves. Circa 1964.*

in a certain way, but the director might feel it is too much and will suggest lowering the pitch or what needs doing to enhance the performance. The director must be clear about the tone of the scene and Tad was vague.

NMK: The Nobel Prize–winning novelist Pearl S. Buck wrote the English screenplay of *Guide* and I believe that was the only screenplay she wrote.

Was your English dialogue dubbed by any chance?

WR: No. I spoke my own lines. I practised them with Pearl S. Buck. She was a very interesting woman. One day she told me: 'Some people may want you to speak in an American accent; don't do that. As long as your lines can be understood, that's all we want. I'll correct you if something isn't right. Don't be self-conscious. If you make a mistake, we can dub it later. Just talk naturally. The film is being shot in India, the story is Indian and, most importantly, the characters are Indian. They're not Americans working in India, so why should Rosie speak in an American accent? It will sound odd.'

NMK: Did you think Rosie was a bold character for the time? Did she break with social norms?

WR: Many people told me I was making a mistake by accepting the role. 'You're shooting yourself in the foot. This will be your last film.' There were many reasons for their concern. The first

(Standing, L to R) Personal hairdresser Mrs Solomon, assistants
John Anderson, Prabhuji Jasbir and actor Anwar Hussain. (Sitting)
Satyadev Dubey and Pearl S. Buck. Photograph taken by Waheeda
Rehman during the filming of the English Guide. *Udaipur, 1963.*

being that when the audience is introduced to Rosie they discover she is a married woman. And a heroine in a Hindi film must be unmarried so that the hero can fall in love with her. On top of that, Rosie leaves her husband and goes off to live with Raju the guide. But they do not marry. This was very bold. Unmarried couples did not live together at the time, and definitely not in Hindi cinema.

I give full credit to Goldie. He treated the story so beautifully and in such a dignified way. The relationship between Raju and Rosie never seemed cheap. In some Hindi films, the other woman is called a '*rakhail*' [mistress] and is portrayed as a vulgar person, more of a vamp type. But Goldie portrayed her in a modern and decent light.

NMK: You're right. Rosie was not at all depicted as an immoral character and is totally unlike the stereotypical heroine of Hindi cinema. She makes her own decisions, is brave enough to refuse to stay in a failed marriage and is unwilling to continue her relationship with Raju when it turns sour.

WR: Exactly! She slaps her husband and walks out on him. A wife reacting like that was never seen in Hindi films. And as you said, when she realizes that Raju is behaving badly—drinking and gambling and using her—she has the courage to walk out on him too.

The characters in *Guide* behave like grown-ups. They believe in mature relationships. Rosie leaves her husband and leaves Raju as well. Their relationship actually starts out of sympathy and only gradually develops into love.

Recently a young woman I met told me she thought the song 'Aaj phir jeene ki tamanna hai' was the first feminist song of Hindi cinema because it describes a woman who takes her life in her own hands. Yes! I want to live.

NMK: An astute observation on the part of that young woman.

Guide won all the top Filmfare Awards in 1967, including the best actress award. In addition, you also won the best actress award for the English version at the Chicago Film Festival in 1965. Did you attend the awards ceremony in the US?

WR: No. In fact I knew nothing about it. It was B.K. Karanjia who called me to ask why I hadn't informed the press about the award. I was quite surprised. He asked me to come and see him in his office. That was the first time I visited the *Filmfare* offices. He showed me an article that had appeared in *Variety*, which read: 'Indian actress Waheeda Rehman wins an award.'

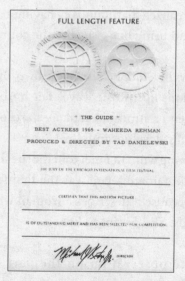

Only later did Waheeda Rehman discover that she had won the best actress award at the Chicago Film Festival in 1965 for the English Guide.

120

Dev never told me about it. Neither did Tad Danielewski. John Anderson, who was an assistant on the film, felt very bad about it all and, very sweetly, he stole the certificate and sent it to me! I didn't make a fuss nor did I mention it to Dev. That wasn't my style.

I have always believed I was very lucky. I was the first Hindi film actress to work with Satyajit Ray and the first Indian actress to win an award in the US.

NMK: Who knows why Dev Anand didn't tell you.

I have never managed to see the English *Guide*, and would really love to some day.

WR: I'm very curious to see it again too. Try and find it for me.

NMK: Of course.

Unlike in the West, where actors are usually contacted through their agents and sent bound scripts, the producer or director in India contacts you directly. Your decision of saying yes or no is based on hearing a narration of the story rather than reading the screenplay.

How does the process of narration work?

WR: The director usually narrated the story to me. Because he wasn't reading from a screenplay, he would come with his chief assistant who would remind him of any detail he might forget while narrating. All actors are narrated the story individually.

We would usually start after lunch and carry on undisturbed until we finished. The director told me the story and described the characters, but did not read any dialogue because the dialogue was often written much later.

Goldie and Gulzar Saab were very good at narration. I remember Rajinder Singh Bedi telling me the story of *Phagun*. Dharmendra, Jaya and Vijay Arora were my co-stars and the film came out in 1973. Bedi Saab was directing but he was also an excellent writer. He told the story well, he even read the dialogue to me. He was a very sensitive man and got emotionally involved and started crying in a sad scene. It was very embarrassing.

Bengali directors like Asit Sen, Moni Bhattacharjee and Basu Bhattacharya were quiet and subdued. Sunil Dutt told the story dramatically and when Dev came to me with the idea of *Prem Pujari*—it was his first film as director—he got very excited. I must admit I was taken aback. *[we laugh]*

NMK: Did you prefer hearing the story or reading a bound script?

WR: I preferred hearing the story first, and then I would have liked to read the script. The screenplay of *Guide* was one of the first screenplays I was given.

I remember Guruduttji asked the author Bimal Mitra to come to Bombay. He read us the story of *Sahib Bibi Aur Ghulam* in his Bengali English. Abrar, Guruduttji and Bimal Mitra worked on the screenplay after that.

NMK: I wonder if you still have any of your old screenplays—*Sahib Bibi Aur Ghulam* or *Guide*? It would be fascinating to read them and to see your notes.

WR: I moved homes so many times and then finally we moved to Bangalore. It's all gone.

Bound scripts were uncommon in the early days. I wish they had been given to us. I would have read the lines repeatedly to become familiar with the dialogue. If you read the script many times, and then do a scene, the words come out sounding far more natural.

I read somewhere that Anthony Hopkins reads his scripts dozens of times. Perhaps that's why his lines flow so easily.

NMK: I wonder if any directors have come to you and said: 'I have written a script only for you.'

WR: They always say that. Of course everyone says: 'Waheedaji, we have written this script only for you.' *[we laugh]*

NMK: Maybe it was true.

WR: Not at all! They repeat the same line to everyone. And in case I wasn't free for some reason, or if there was a money issue and I couldn't do the film, then they'd promptly go to another actress and say: 'We have written this script only for you.'

NMK: I am sure they did write the script only for you in some cases. I doubt they were fibbing all the time!

But tell me, when you heard the narration, did you have a good instinct about which story would make a good film?

WR: I made mistakes, but usually I had a pretty good idea of what would work. I instantly knew about *Guide*. I had read the book and when I read the script, I thought to myself: 'Wow, this is going to be good.'

I never think about the commercial success of a movie. You have to make the movie in the best way you know how. No one knows how the film will turn out or how it will be received. When David Lean made *Doctor Zhivago*, could he have imagined that his next film, *Ryan's Daughter*, would not appeal as much? It may have been a good movie but people were not crazy about it.

If any producer were able to predict the success of a film then he would be God! Everyone would go rushing to him and ask him if their films will succeed at the box office. No one anywhere in the world really knows what will work for an audience. And that's part of the excitement of making movies.

When I was making *Khamoshi* in the late sixties some people asked why I was acting in a film with such a heavy subject, a subject they thought no one would like. But I personally liked the story as well as the character I played—a nurse called Radha. I did not think about how well the film would do. What mattered to me was feeling strongly about the subject.

NMK: Did the final film ever match the story narration?

WR: No, never! But that's to be expected. Directors have to make changes during the various stages of production.

The dialogue was always changing. Many times the scene was given to us on the day of the shoot. On the spot! The assistant director would hand us a bit of paper on which the dialogue was written, and we would start memorizing the lines. Then he would come back and say: 'The scene has changed, don't memorize those lines.' Oh my God, now to memorize new ones!

There were even times when the dialogue was written shot by shot. Even after we had filmed a scene, the director decided to change a line here or there and we had to go for another take.

This is how we all worked—Nargisji, Meena Kumari, Dilip Saab, Balraj Sahni, Nutan and all the others. In spite of that, we didn't do too badly, did we? *[smiles]*

NMK: Far from it! Your generation set the bar high for acting in Indian cinema.

I am curious to know if there is a performance you like above all others?

*With (L to R) O.P. Ralhan, Meena Kumari, Mrs Kewal Singh, Nargis,
Geeta Singh and her father, Ambassador Kewal Singh, in Moscow
during the 1967 film festival where* Teesri Kasam *was screened.*

WR: I don't watch my old films. If I happen to see one, I am
very critical. The acting, the hairstyle, the clothes—I think it's
all very bad. I always feel I could have done better.

Recently there was a programme in Ahmedabad where my
work was discussed. They played a scene from *Aadmi* and when
I saw the clip I thought I hadn't done too badly. But rarely do
I think I've done well.

NMK: When dubbing became the norm in Hindi cinema, actors
had a second chance of enhancing their performance through

re-recording their lines. Until the late 1960s, films were being made in sync sound, which favours more naturalistic acting.

What did you prefer? Dubbing or sync sound?

WR: Filming in sync sound is by far the best way of working. You can put in real effort, shot by shot.

When we were dubbing, we worked on the scene as a whole and it's easy to miss the finer nuances of a shot. Filming in sync sound meant paying greater attention to your lines in every shot.

I found it very difficult recreating the emotion and mood when I started dubbing because I was used to working in sync sound. If the lip movement matched, the emotion didn't, and when I got the emotion right the lip movement was out of sync. I had to concentrate hard to match the mood of the scene that I might have shot months earlier.

But finally it didn't take long to grasp what was needed once I got used to dubbing. Basically you had to keep three things in mind: the mood, the lip movement and the emotion.

I am very pleased Hindi films are being shot in sync sound again. For years Hindi films were dubbed and I didn't enjoy working like that.

NMK: I think sound can enhance a sense of reality on screen and I am sure dubbing added substantially to the artificiality of some Hindi films.

Often there isn't much sound perspective either. Obvious

examples are when you see a busy outdoor scene and the voices of the actors have the clarity of a quiet studio recording. Or the actor's voice sounds so close to the mike, even when he or she is in a wide shot. Dubbing increased the split between the actor's physical presence and the voice.

WR: That's right.

I think we actors also concentrated better when working in sync sound. It imposed a certain discipline on the set, and though there were 100 or 150 people around—the spot boys, the light boys, the focus pullers, the make-up assistants, the hairstylists, etc.—they went silent when the director shouted: 'Start action! Roll sound!' Everyone stood perfectly still.

NMK: As you were saying, you did not have the script in advance, so I assume there was no chance of researching a character.

WR: How could we? I worked on three movies a month—ten days on one film, a week on another and six days on a third. I'd have a few days' break in between. Where was the time to do any research?

I believe Dustin Hoffman spent days with autistic people before making *Rain Man*. Hollywood actors have that luxury because they get bound scripts and have the time to prepare thoroughly for a role. They also work on one film at a time. This is not how we used to work.

Of course, I know things are changing and some actors in

A chance meeting with south Indian star Padmini at the Hyderabad airport. Circa 1960.

India have started researching their roles. I read that Farhan Akhtar spent a lot of time researching his part as Milkha Singh in *Bhaag Milkha Bhaag*.

NMK: Did an idea of how to develop a character ever come to you in a dream?

WR: Not really. But I have taken inspiration from the behaviour of someone I know. I was acting in a TV serial [*Katha Sagar*] by Shyam Benegal, which was based on Guy de Maupassant's short stories. I played a lonely Christian woman from Goa. She is relentlessly pursued by an estate agent who wants to get her house somehow. Knowing this woman is very fond of drinking, he keeps bringing her feni. I wondered how I was going to act this part because I don't drink alcohol.

My husband, Shashi, and I used to spend a lot of time with Salim Khan and I noticed he would make a gulping sound when he was drinking. I imitated that gulping sound in the shot. Shyam was taken aback and asked: 'How did you do that?' I explained to him it was Salim Saab of Salim–Javed who had inspired me. *[laughs]*

NMK: Considering the fact that you would sometimes be given the scene at the last minute, what kind of scenes did you enjoy playing? Romantic? Sad or light scenes?

WR: I liked playing romantic scenes and light scenes too. People liked me in romantic scenes. I have a very serious face, not a *chulbuli* [mischievous] face. I thought I could do light scenes quite well. My acting wasn't too bad in *Ram Aur Shyam*, *Aadmi* and in a few scenes in films like *Patthar Ke Sanam* and *Ek Phool Char Kaante*.

NMK: When you were filming a reaction shot, did your co-stars stand in?

WR: Many did. Dilip Saab, Sunil Dutt, Dev Anand and Rajendra Kumar always stood in. Hearing their tone helped me get the right expression in the reaction shot.

If my co-star was away from the set, an assistant would read the lines to me. We had such amusing assistants—they read the lines without any emotion whatsoever—and everyone would laugh because I performed very badly.

NMK: You have worked with a variety of actors and directors, and with some directors like Yash Chopra you played both heroine and mother in his films. What were his strengths as a director?

WR: He was a master at portraying romance on the screen, and his technical execution was very good.

I remember Yashji came to see me about *Kabhi Kabhie*. When I heard the story, I agreed to do the film. Then Gulshan Rai, the producer of *Deewaar*, a film that Yashji was also directing, asked him to offer me the role of the mother—the role Nirupa

Roy eventually played. I told Yashji: 'I don't mind doing it. The mother in *Deewaar* has a few good scenes and in any case I am not the romantic lead in *Kabhi Kabhie*, and so why not play the mother?'

Yashji thought otherwise and advised me to say no—he said how could I play Amitabh Bachchan's mother in *Deewaar*, if I was playing his wife in *Kabhi Kabhie*? He reminded me both films were going to be released at more or less the same time, but added if Gulshan Rai were to ask me I should say I was the one who had refused the *Deewaar* role. *[smiles]*

NMK: Was there any director you wish you had worked with?

WR: Bimal Roy. His production company offered me a role but it was going to be made by another director. I would have liked to work with Mehboob Saab too.

My husband and Saira Banu were cast in Mehboob Saab's last film *Habba Khatoon*, but when Mehboob Khan passed away in 1964, the film was shelved.

I was keen to work with Hrishikesh Mukherjee. We were travelling on a flight together and were sitting next to each other. He said he had read a story he wanted to adapt and thought the lead role would suit me. I was very happy. I expected him to get in touch but heard nothing. I believe he told someone he had offered me a role, and it was I who had not called him. I didn't realize I was supposed to call.

NMK: Some actors have a reputation of being difficult and fussy and having tantrums on set. Were you ever like that?

WR: *[smiles]* I was most dutiful.

The first time I worked with Raj Kapoor was in *Ek Dil Sao Afsane*—R.C. Talwar was directing. We were shooting in someone's bungalow. Rajji came late as usual, and then didn't want to start filming. We asked him: 'What is it, Rajji? The whole unit is waiting, what are you doing?' He said: 'I am not in the mood. Sorry.' The owner of the bungalow was a friend of Rajji's and had the courage to tell him: 'You are paid to get into the mood, my dear. Please get into the mood and start filming.'

My personal hairdresser Mrs Solomon would sometimes say: 'They make you wait for hours, why don't you make a fuss? Why don't you complain?' I used to tell her: 'I am paid from 9.30 to 6.30. If they don't call me for a shot, they're wasting their time and not mine.'

Mrs Solomon was with me for ten years and when I had more or less stopped working, she moved to America to join her sisters who had settled there. She has passed away but her family still lives in the States.

NMK: If you had to wait on set for hours, what did you do?

WR: I read. But if it was past 6.30, I felt I had the right to ask what was going on. Are you going to take my shot today?

Sometimes the director would say: '*Jam nahin raha hai.*

[It isn't working.] Let's call it a day. We can sit and have tea together.' That kind of thing happened too.

I am reminded of an incident during the shooting of *Patthar Ke Sanam*. We actors knew the director Raja Nawathe was not a very forceful man and could be easily bullied. Manoj Kumar, Pran, Mehmood and I got together and decided to pull his leg. We took the producer A.A. Nadiadwala into our confidence and said we were going to have some *masti* [fun] and upset the director.

When the director had placed the camera into position and the lighting was ready, he asked us to rehearse the shot. First Pran, looking furious, told Raja Nawathe: 'Dada, I'm Pran after all! What is this? My back is the only thing you can see in the shot. I am sorry, I don't like it at all. You must change the angle.' The director asked for the camera position and lighting to be changed. It took almost an hour.

When the shot was ready, Manoj Kumar said: 'Hello! I'm the leading man. How can I enter the shot like that?' One after the other, we took turns making some kind of fuss. Raja didn't know what to do. Then we all burst out laughing. The poor director!

Sometimes we misbehaved on the set, but today there is no way you can do that because there is too much money involved.

NMK: The budgets are enormous now and it would be difficult to delay a shoot for fun. But what if an actor just can't get the emotion right?

WR: It can be a struggle. When I used to set off for the studio in the mornings, I knew the scene I was going to shoot, and would try to get myself into the right frame of mind.

Being prepared isn't sometimes enough. I was shooting an emotional scene with Nirupa Roy for *Mujhe Jeene Do*, but neither of us got it right. We filled our eyes with glycerin, and so it appeared we were crying, but the emotion wasn't there. We were phoney and artificial and giggling under our breath. We tried very hard but nothing worked. Finally we asked the director Moni Bhattacharjee for a short break.

Nirupa and I sat outside the set. After a few minutes, I said: 'I think I've been doing too many emotional scenes in the past month. I feel empty.'

'You are absolutely right. I feel the same.' Nirupa and I realized we had become drained of feelings and needed a few days' break from playing highly charged scenes.

There is a limit to your ability of expressing real emotions no matter how fine an actor you are. You may be acting, but you also need to feel something as a person.

NMK: It shows on screen when a performance is heartfelt. I am thinking of you as Radha in *Khamoshi*.

WR: The director Asit Sen was very good and the only time I worked with him was in *Khamoshi*. He had made many Bengali and Hindi movies, including *Mamta*. I liked him very much because he was a sensitive man and had a great understanding of cinema. He guided me to deliver the right tone.

NMK: Many people confuse the director Asit Sen with the comedian Asit Sen. But they were entirely different people. The director Asit Sen was a former assistant to Bimal Roy and came from Calcutta with Bimal Roy and his team to live in Bombay in 1950.

Apparently *Khamoshi* was the Hindi version of the 1959 Bengali film *Deep Jweley Jai* that Asit Sen made with Suchitra Sen in the role of the psychiatric nurse that you ultimately played. Was it a tough role?

WR: *Khamoshi* was a demanding film and so was the role. The character I played, Radha, had intense but suppressed feelings. She has great self-control and was not the kind of person to demand that the man she loves must love her in return. It would be out of character for her to behave like that. Acting quieter emotions is far more difficult.

On the other hand when I played Chamelijaan in *Mujhe Jeene Do*, I was required to express loud emotions. She starts off as a *tawaif* and later becomes a dacoit's wife. She yells and shouts. That kind of behaviour suited the character and background she came from.

NMK: Did rehearsals help you achieve the right pitch of performance? Did you have camera rehearsals?

WR: No, not in the early days. Before we put on our costumes and did our make-up, all the artistes were called on the set and the director would explain the camera positions. This was about rehearsing movement, not performance.

Say an actor had to walk over and sit on a chair while talking. We would then rehearse just that movement and not necessarily the whole scene. The idea was to get familiar with our cues and make us feel comfortable. They call it 'blocking the scene'.

NMK: Actors talk of becoming the character; was it something you believed in?

WR: Yes. I became Gulaabo [*Pyaasa*] or Shanti [*Kaagaz Ke Phool*]. I think I knew how to act but relied on the director to help me stay in character throughout the story: '*Shanti aise nahin karegi. Shanti aise hi karegi.*' [Shanti would not do this. Shanti would do that.] Consistency in performance is important.

NMK: You're right. We've got to believe that when we meet someone on the screen, they are the same person from the first to the last scene. That can be tricky when a film has a lot of dialogue. Do you think Hindi films tend to overdo the talking?

WR: Indian films are too verbose. There's too much talking. I have told my writers and directors many times: 'Saab, this whole scene is a repeat. Why don't you cut it down?' But they didn't listen to me.

I think emotions expressed through songs and music are a good way of taking the story forward. They're emotionally more effective than endless dialogue.

NMK: I think Hindi film songs are the glue that binds us to Indian cinema, especially the old songs—they are the most original aspect. It's interesting that the audience tolerates the repetition of storyline, but they will not tolerate the same song being used again and again.

That said, songs today have less purpose in the story. I am sure you agree they don't seem to fit in the current mood of today's films.

WR: Well, they don't fit because the stories are often action-based or they have more realistic settings. Everyone wants special effects these days. In the realistic dramas or the crime thrillers, they tend to use the song as a background song—not a lip-synced song.

I think that's because the characters in some recent films would look too odd if they were singing. You can't expect the hero in *The Lunchbox* or *Paan Singh Tomar* to sing a song, can you? How could the character Vidya Balan plays in *Kahaani* sing? It would look totally wrong.

There are also fewer situations in the stories today for the characters to sing. In a way I think it is a good thing.

In our time songs were used to express love. But now the couple meet and are hugging and kissing soon enough—where's the time or opportunity for them to sing a love song?

NMK: I suppose it would be out of place for a hero to also sing praise of the heroine's beautiful eyes—her '*nargisi ankhen*'—when she is scantily clad. I am not sure why would he concentrate on her eyes? *[we laugh]*

We see comedies, action stories and crime thrillers dominate film-going tastes in the 2010s. I wonder if romance has finally taken a back seat today. Is it a loss for Indian cinema?

WR: There has to be change. You can't stick to the same themes like love and tragedy. People are changing in India. The audiences are more educated, otherwise would they accept films like *Kahaani* or *Paan Singh Tomar* or *Kai Po Che!*? These films have done well at the box office and so show us that the audience is changing.

In my era, people who watched films were not highly educated. Perhaps that's why melodramas and weepy love stories dominated our films. Those films struck a chord, and people would let out their frustrations by watching them.

Audiences today have a lot more entertainment. They're far more aware because of the vast number of television channels and the Net. Little kids can teach you a lot today.

NMK: Earlier films were indeed preoccupied by romantic themes, and this was particularly true of your era. Do you think the prevalence of arranged marriages had something to do with it?

WR: I think so. We should not generalize, but even today some traditional families, especially in small towns and villages, do not want the couple to know each other before marriage. The girl does not see the boy's face before her wedding day. The poor thing doesn't even know what he looks like. Is he hideous or handsome or what?

This was the norm in earlier times and so there had to be a sense of frustration and anxiety of not knowing who they will live with for the rest of their lives. Young people have a yearning for love and this increased the appeal of romantic stories. The story of doomed lovers like Laila–Majnu, Heer–Raanjha and others were always popular and so it was natural that romance of all kinds would become central to our films.

Our society is changing and that's why you see a wider variety of film subjects.

NMK: Like film stories, as we said, the role of songs is also changing and they don't have the same importance as before. I think it would be a loss if they disappeared entirely from Hindi films. They made Indian cinema unique.

In addition to performing and delivering dialogue, there is an art to lip-syncing. Did you find it difficult to mime to the words of a playback singer?

WR: Dilip Saab would tease me because I would actually sing along with the playback track. One can tell if the actor is singing or not. *[sings]* 'Kabhi kabhi mere dil mein'. I may be singing out

With sisters Shahida (left) and Sayeeda with whom she continues to share a very close relationship. 1960s.

of tune, but you can see the neck veins protrude slightly—that's how you know if I'm singing.

The basic requirement is to know the song perfectly. You need to feel and understand the meaning of words and only then can you have the right facial expressions to match the words and mood of the song.

In a song like 'Jaane kya tu ne kahi', it was nearly all about facial expressions. There was a little body movement—the way I walk, the way I look at the hero, flirt and seduce him—all that was important.

'Waqt ne kiya kya haseen situm' on the other hand is played in the background. I do not mime to the track and so I relied entirely on silent expressions—my face had to say it all. There was no movement in the song. I sit in a chair and knit. At one point, the souls of the two characters walk across the studio floor and merge together in a dissolve—a merging of shadows.

NMK: That was an extraordinary moment—an imaginary union or one could say a union of spirits. It is almost ghostly.

WR: It was very unusual. By and large, movement in a song varies according to the situation in the story.

NMK: There are many examples of excellent song picturizations but do you think that background music has been used well in Hindi cinema?

WR: I think it is rarely used well. The songs have a definite purpose and take the story forward. They are a form of narrative through lyrics and music. The old songs were very good. But you can't say the same about the background music. It was often too loud and too present.

I liked the way S.D. Burman and Madan Mohan composed background music. I never had the opportunity of working in a film in which the music was composed by Madan Mohan. But he was good. O.P. Nayyar did not write music for many movies, but his background scores were very effective—especially in the early crime thrillers like *Aar Paar* and *C.I.D.* I liked his music in those films.

NMK: I read an interview with Meena Kumari in which she said she didn't have to act if Lata Mangeshkar was singing for her. I am sure she meant the emotional power of Lataji's singing was enough, so why act when the voice conveyed all the feelings?

Did the way Lata Mangeshkar sing help you find the right way of expressing the song?

WR: No matter how much one praises Lataji, it isn't enough. She is a perfectionist. She takes her work totally seriously. Many other singers have come and gone. But she is unmatched.

It's an absolute fact that her singing helped us actresses a lot. The feelings of a song came through her voice while she kept something of the personality of the actress. When you heard a song, without seeing the film in which it appeared, you could tell if Lataji was singing for Meena Kumari, Nargis, Madhubala or Nutan. When she sang for Dimple in *Bobby*, her voice had the innocence of a fifteen-year-old. Matching the voice with the face is very important or else the performance itself cannot convince anyone.

Lataji is a great artist and yet so down to earth. I remember we were in Sunil Dutt's Ajanta Arts Welfare Troupe show in Bangladesh in 1972. A whole group of artistes had gone for the show. Lataji and I were sharing a room. One day I had undressed, and was about to have my bath when I realized that there was no running water. She understood my predicament and immediately rushed off and found a bucket, filled it with water and carried it back to me. She had no pretensions whatsoever.

Nargisji, Lataji and I laughed a lot together. We had wonderful times.

NMK: One of Lataji's songs for you is the famous 'Aaj phir jeene ki tamanna hai' from *Guide*. How did that song get made?

WR: We were filming in Udaipur when Dev went to Bombay to record the song. He returned worried, and told Goldie he was unhappy with the song that Burmanda had given him. He didn't like it at all and wondered what had come over Dada. They got on very well and Dev knew Dada would not mind if he were asked to compose another number in its place.

But we all insisted we should at least hear the song, and when we heard it, we loved it. We told Dev: 'What's wrong with you? It's a beautiful song. It will fit perfectly into the story. The music

With Lata Mangeshkar with whom she shares many years of friendship.
Photograph courtesy: Lata Mangeshkar.

is good and Lataji's singing—everything about it is good.' But Dev kept saying he didn't like it.

Goldie persuaded Dev to let him at least film the song. He explained that when we returned to Bombay we could view the rushes and if Dev still didn't like it, we could come back to Udaipur and film another song in its place. Dev agreed and we started filming.

The song was shot over five days at various locations in Rajasthan. Every evening when the crew returned to the hotel, Dev noticed they were all humming the tune. On the fifth day, he said: 'Sorry, I made a mistake. It's a lovely song. We don't need to record another.'

Before the song starts, there is a short exchange between Raju and Rosie in which Raju says: 'Yesterday you seemed like a forty-year-old woman, disenchanted and tired with life, and today you are like a sixteen-year-old, carefree and happy.'

'Aaj phir jeene ki tamanna hai' is the answer to Raju's lines. The song had such a feeling of freedom and much of the credit goes to Lataji. Her singing matched Rosie's emotions perfectly. It made me really feel the words: 'Today I want to live again; today I want to die.'

When talking about the difference between old and new songs, Lataji once said: 'The orchestra was there to give us singers a rest. Today we singers are there to give the orchestra a rest!' *[laughs]*

NMK: I suppose what she meant was that the music is more important today than the lyrics—because songs are now essentially dance numbers.

WR: Even the dance numbers don't show real dancing. The dances are more like PT drills. When I listen to recent film songs, they all sound the same to me. They have a good rhythm, but it is the same rhythm again and again.

NMK: Another lovely and unusual song is 'Bhanwaraa badaa nadaan haye' from *Sahib Bibi Aur Ghulam*, sung by Asha Bhonsle for you.

WR: She's another great artiste. She brought that song alive. If you hear it again, you will notice how she stresses each syllable. 'Bhan-wa-ra bad-aa naa-daan . . .' etc. I had to make exaggerated facial movements to match her singing and intonation. She sang the words like that because in the scene Jabba is making fun of Bhoothnath who she thinks is foolish. Ashaji understood Jabba's character and the situation in the story totally.

How beautifully she sang 'Nadi naare na jaao shyaam paiyyan padun' in *Mujhe Jeene Do* and 'Paan khaaye saiyyan hamaaro' in *Teesri Kasam*.

You know, the singer I used to meet very often was Rafi Saab because we appeared in many stage shows together. He had a magical voice and was a very simple and good man. When he sang, you could also guess who he was singing for—Dev Anand, Balraj Sahni or Dilip Kumar. Looking at the shy and reserved

147

Rafi Saab, you could never imagine it was he who sang those wild songs for Shammi Kapoor.

NMK: Shammi Kapoor had such rhythm and abandon. I think that, among today's stars, Hrithik Roshan is the best dancer—a naturally gifted dancer.

But I suppose most actors need only give the impression they can dance because their dance steps have to last for a few seconds on the screen. Then the shot is cut. More than the actor, I think, the film editor is doing the dancing today. *[we laugh]*

Your dancing was of an exceptionally high standard. Can you tell me how you prepared for a dance scene?

WR: I insisted on rehearsing for at least five days with my choreographer to avoid wasting time on the day of the shoot.

The director explained the camera movements to me so I would know beforehand if he had decided to start the dance with a trolley movement or a wide shot.

Most of my dances were filmed in extended shots with no cuts. I was used to dancing for two hours at a stretch for the stage. So giving an extended take was no problem for me.

NMK: You have worked with many choreographers. Did you have any favourite?

WR: I liked many of them, but I think I worked with Hiralal the most. For *Guide* I told Dev I wanted both B. Hiralal and his elder brother B. Sohanlal who was a Kathak expert. They were originally from Jaipur and had settled in Madras many years ago. They spoke Tamil and Telugu, but basically were Rajasthanis. Hiralal's granddaughter Vaibhavi Merchant is a well-known choreographer today.

I lost touch with Sohanlal and Hiralal over the years, and when I started playing character roles, there was no need for me to sing and dance.

NMK: Hiralal was responsible for choreographing many brilliant songs, including 'Inhi logon ne' in *Pakeezah* and 'Piya tose naina lage re' in *Guide*.

But one of Hindi cinema's most memorable dances is your extraordinary snake dance in *Guide*. It was full of emotion and dramatic tension without the help of lyrics. It must have been a difficult dance to perform.

WR: I tell you, Hiralal broke my bones. We rehearsed in a sound studio in Dadar between five and eight in the morning. Then I'd come home, have a bath and go to another studio to shoot some dialogue scenes. Straight from there I went back to the dance rehearsal and we'd work till ten or eleven at night.

My God! It killed me. I couldn't walk for days and it was only with great difficulty that I managed to get out of my car because all my muscles were aching so much. My driver Naseer Ahmed said: '*Memsaab, ye kaisa zaalim aadmi hai. Aap ki jaan nikaal dete hai.*' [Madam, he's a cruel fellow. He's killing you.]

NMK: But it was well worth it! I am curious about the girl who danced with you. She was fantastic. Who was she?

WR: Hiralalji's assistant, Sheela. She was very good and graceful. I told her to become a solo dancer. But she had her own logic and said: 'I won't get many solo dances, but as an assistant I can work in ten pictures.' I saw Sheela in some film recently but haven't met her for years. She was excellent and so was Saroj Khan who was Sohanlalji's assistant.

NMK: Did Vijay Anand choose the camera positions for the snake dance or was it Hiralal?

WR: Goldie was a very good director and always decided the camera positions. He left the choreography to Hiralal.

NMK: Do tell me about that fantastic circular shot that comes at the end of the snake dance. How was that done?

WR: In those days, we didn't have crab trolleys and the cameras were bulky and heavy. In the middle of the set at Mehboob Studio, they built a raised platform on which the camera and circular tracks were placed. They call this structure a '*ghoda*' [horse]. Fali Mistry, his assistant and Goldie sat there with the camera tilted down for the top shot.

I danced round and round and the camera followed me on the circular tracks. At the end of the take, I felt really dizzy. There was a camera assistant who ran alongside the tracks, holding all the cables—we both went round and round—it must have looked like a jalebi being fried. *[we laugh]*

NMK: Wow! Vijay Anand and Fali Mistry were very inventive. That dance will remain forever as among the best Hindi film dances ever.

WR: You know the greatest compliment I got was during the making of Yash Chopra's *Lamhe*. There is a scene in the film in which Anil Kapoor slaps Sridevi when she tells him she loves him. She is upset and in her frustration she dances.

I was in London for the shoot of *Lamhe* and Sridevi was yet to arrive. When she came, she told me: '*Yashji mera dimaag kha gayen ke tum Waheeda ka snake dance dekh ke London aana.*' [Yashji drove me crazy. He kept saying I must see Waheeda's snake dance before coming to London.]

Sridevi danced in a similar style but it didn't work that well. The frustration she feels and Rosie's frustration come from different emotions. I don't know if they finally kept her dance in *Lamhe*.

NMK: Yes, Sridevi's dance was in the film. Can you tell me what form of dance was the snake dance?

WR: You can't call it Bharatanatyam or Kathak. It is a mix of all forms. But it had proper mudras and footwork.

Film dancing is a blend of Indian dances, developed especially for a film. Sometimes you change a movement to make it look good on the screen.

NMK: You mean dance movements are designed for the frame?

WR: Yes, especially in a close-up. A dance movement must have a graceful shape and not go outside the frame. If you're filming a movement in a wide or a mid shot, the movement does not need to be so precise.

Directors who did not know about rhythm and music usually left the camera positions and framing to the choreographer. The director would sit on the set and watch—unlike Guru Dutt who always decided the camera movement. He had learned dance under Uday Shankar and knew all about choreography.

NMK: I am sure working with Uday Shankar must have helped Guru Dutt define his style when it came to filming dance sequences. Minoo Mumtaz performed some unforgettable songs in Guru Dutt's films. I am thinking of 'Saaqiya aaj mujhe neend nahin aayegi' [in *Sahib Bibi Aur Ghulam*]. I asked Murthy why the chorus dancers were filmed in shadow. And he said, because they were ugly, they decided not to show their faces.

WR: I don't think that's true. *[laughs]* The song had such beautiful lighting. The film was set at the end of the nineteenth century, and I thought the lighting effect helped create the shadows made by those old-fashioned *pankhas* [swinging ceiling fans pulled by rope].

Minoo Mumtaz was excellent in that song. She was a very nice person. Her brother, the comedian Mehmood, once asked me to work opposite him in some movie. I gave him some excuse about not having the time. He got so annoyed with me that in one of his films he tells a girl: 'Hey, Waheeda Rehman, what are you doing? Are you washing dishes like a maid?' It was very mean of him. *[we laugh]*

He was a very talented actor and changed his personality in every film. Johnny Walker was always Johnny, but that was not true of Mehmood.

NMK: Which male actors do you think danced well?

WR: In my time the heroes didn't dance as such. There was Bhagwan, and among the romantic heroes I believe it was Jeetendra who started the trend of the dancing hero.

In a love song the couple would usually hold hands, or run through fields. So no dance steps were required. I may be wrong but I think Dilip Kumar danced for the first time in *Gunga Jumna*. There is such charm in his whole personality. He is very lovable, sweet and nice. He has a lovely smile.

I made four films with him, *Dil Diya Dard Liya, Aadmi, Ram Aur Shyam* and *Mashaal*. But my role in *Mashaal* was very small. I didn't like *Dil Diya Dard Liya*. It was too melodramatic. The director made us cry too much. I feel dramatic situations should make the audience cry, not the actors.

Personally I liked Dilip Kumar in *Gunga Jumna, Andaz* and *Daag. Amar* was interesting too. His voice and his effortless acting are impressive. He has a lot of depth and expression in his eyes—Dilip Kumar is a natural actor like Motilal, Balraj Sahni and Rehman.

NMK: You would be in the same group of natural actors. You have created many lifelike personalities on the screen. The fact that you underplayed your roles has helped your films not feel dated. Much more than dialogue or editing, I think performance can really date a film. When you see some old films, an actor's wooden performance is what gets the audience laughing. Nothing dates as badly, not the music, photography or even editing.

In this current generation, I find that Nawazuddin Siddiqui is a natural. He's brilliant. I hope the attention he is now getting doesn't corrupt him.

WR: His performances are so different from each other. He doesn't emote through facial expressions; his feelings come from the inside. He's very good. In *The Lunchbox*, there is a wonderful scene where Nawaz's character is feeling hurt and snubbed by the character Irrfan Khan is playing. You can sense Nawaz's feelings in his slightest glance and gesture. He is subtle and moving.

NMK: For the record, I'd like to ask if you had worked in many films that were never released.

WR: There were a few—there was a film with Rajesh Khanna and Tina Munim called *Baayein Haath Ka Khel*, an NFDC [National Film Development Corporation of India] film called *Trisandhya* and *Ulfat*. I don't know if *Trisandhya* was finally released.

NMK: Your Wikipedia entry has *Baayein Haath Ka Khel* down as a released film.

WR: I am sure it was never released. I think there was some misunderstanding between the producer and Rajesh Khanna. I don't know what happened in the end because I had moved to Bangalore.

Rajesh Khanna and I acted in a few films together—*Khamoshi*, *Maqsad* and *Dharam Kanta*.

NMK: He was amazingly popular in his time. His smile became a kind of trademark.

I have always believed a star must have a winning smile. Rajesh Khanna's smile had millions swooning and so did Dev Anand's. You have that kind of smile too—a smile that lights up the face.

WR: Oh yes? Madhubala had a lovely smile. Dev Anand was all charm.

In fact he was the only star who could put his arms around any actress and she would not object or push him away. Today the stars are physically affectionate with each other—there's a lot of hugging—but we were reserved in our time. Yet none of us minded when Dev put his arms around us. He would say: 'Hi, Waheeda! Hi, Nandu'—that's what he used to call Nanda.

The other actors were jealous and complained that whenever they tried to give us a hug, we girls would push them away. Dev was a decent flirt. *[laughs]*

NMK: Your family background, being the daughter of an IAS officer, was probably quite different from the background of most people working in films in the 1950s. Was it something that set you apart?

WR: Not really, all kinds of people worked in films. When I first started, I was very apprehensive and my mother was too. But I never forgot the advice of our producer friend Mr Prasad who said I should not concede to every demand. For example, I made it a rule that no one should call me at home after 9.30 at night.

Sometime in 1965, I was working in *Palki.* One evening K. Asif was finalizing a scene with the actor Mahesh Kaul and the writers of the film. At 11 p.m. they told their production assistant to inform me of the schedule. The assistant immediately said:

'No, sir, we cannot call Waheedaji at home after 9.30.' Asif Saab couldn't believe it.

A few days later, he asked me: 'I want to know if it's true that no one can call you after 9.30? Why not?'

'Asif Saab, I am not afraid of hard work, but there must be some discipline. Only my sisters who live out of town or my close friends can call me after 9.30.'

NMK: K. Asif was an amazingly accomplished film-maker. What do you remember of him?

WR: If anyone talks of Asif Saab, the first thing they speak about is his style of smoking. It was so distinctive. He kept his cigarette between his third and fourth finger, clicked his fingers and took a deep drag.

When we were working in *Palki*, I noticed that Asif Saab did not instruct us clearly about what he wanted us to do. He did not speak in full sentences. The actors had to know him well to second-guess what he wanted. When we were ready for the take, Asif Saab would just say: 'Try . . . with force.'

'Do you mean the emotions should be more forceful? Louder?'

'Yes, that's what I said.' He'd click his fingers and take another drag.

In the beginning I found it difficult to understand him. Rajendra Kumar, who was my co-star in *Palki*, had to explain what Asif Saab meant to say. It was very amusing.

NMK: I suppose some people with a strong visual sense cannot always describe what they want in words. He was probably seeing the scene in his mind's eye and could not articulate it.

WR: This is true. He was imaginative and fabulous at conceiving scenes. I don't believe he was very educated or anything like that, but then one does not have to rely on intellect or education in the creative arts—all you need is imagination. I think creativity is an inborn gift.

Asif Saab once told us about a scene he wanted in *Mughal-e-Azam* where Prince Saleem sends a love letter to Anaarkali. He asked the writers Kamaal Amrohi and Vajahat Mirza to come up with a romantic idea, but they couldn't. Then Asif Saab came up with the idea of wrapping Saleem's letter in a lotus and letting the flower float to Anaarkali through the waterways of the palace. How exquisite!

While we were working on *Palki*, Asif Saab narrated some fantastic scenes of *Sasta Khoon Mehenga Paani*, a film he was planning with Rajendra Kumar. Sadly the film was shelved. He was a very interesting person.

NMK: I wonder why he was not credited as the director of *Palki* along with S.U. Sunny and Mahesh Kaul.

WR: S.U. Sunny was to produce and direct the film but he passed away in 1966. Then sometime later Rajendra thought they should restart it because it was a very good subject. Mahesh

Kaul was the original screenplay writer, and he decided to direct, but Rajendra Kumar wanted K. Asif. So Asif Saab helped out on an informal basis and maybe that's why it was agreed that he would not be credited.

There was a lot of confusion on the *Palki* sets. It isn't easy working with two directors. They were both very intelligent men and we actors didn't know who to listen to. Mahesh Kaul would say the take was good and Asif Saab would say let's go for another take.

NMK: Your co-star Rajendra Kumar was a popular actor in the 1960s and part of the '70s. As you know he was famously called 'Jubilee Kumar' because many of his films enjoyed a jubilee run. I believe you made three films with him.

WR: Besides *Palki*, I made *Shatranj* and *Dharti* with him. He was a very popular star. But he cried a lot in his films. I used to tell him: 'If you cry so much, Rajendraji, how will I cry?' He would smile and say: 'Oh sorry, you're right. One more take.'

I remember this one delightful incident. Rajendra and I were on location in Lausanne during the shooting of *Dharti* in the late 1960s and by chance I met a little Swiss German girl in a restaurant. When she saw me, she came over and sat on my lap and refused to go back to her parents who were at another table. She would not leave my side for a minute. Her parents had to go somewhere and so they left, saying they'd be back to collect her in a few hours.

During the shooting of Dharti *in Lausanne, a young Swiss German girl (unidentified) took a shine to Waheeda Rehman. Circa 1970.*

The little girl spoke no English and I couldn't speak German, but we somehow communicated through hand gestures. We had a lovely time. At the end of the day when her parents came to take her home, she was very upset to leave me. She was a sweet little girl. Rajendra Kumar was most amused by the whole story and said the girl and I must have some connection from a previous lifetime. I don't know her name but I have not forgotten her.

NMK: The world has become such a small place, thanks to the Net, that she might find herself in this book some day! That would be nice.

Were you considered a romantic pair with Rajendra Kumar?

WR: Not really. Meena Kumari and Rajendra Kumar made a very successful romantic screen pair and worked in many hit films with tragic stories. Rajendra Kumar was so popular.

Dharmendra also had a great following. And many people loved Balraj Sahni. He was such a sensitive artist and had a lovely face.

NMK: His face epitomized decency and integrity, and what an extraordinary actor he was.

Can we talk about another fascinating director you worked with—the exuberant Manmohan Desai?

WR: Before we made *Coolie* in 1983, he was making *Naseeb* and that's when we met. For a party scene in the film where Amitabh sings 'John Jaani Janaardhan', Manmohan Desai asked many top Hindi film stars to make a guest appearance. He also asked me to participate. I think it was the first and probably the last time that so many stars came together in the same film.

On the day of the shoot, Manmohan Desai said: 'Waheedaji, I have a request; I am sure you won't refuse. Shammi Kapoor wants to walk into the party arm in arm with you.' I said okay and he ran like a child to tell Shammiji, who had wanted to work with me, but somehow it had never happened.

Shammiji came over to me and said: '*Arey kya baat hai ji?*

I was dying to work with you.' I said: 'This is our last chance. Let's enter the party together.'

Sometime later, Manmohan Desai offered me the role of Amitabh's mother in *Coolie*. He asked Shashi [Rekhy] to play my husband in the film. But Shashi had given up acting ten years before that and wasn't keen to face the camera again.

NMK: *Coolie* became doubly famous because of Amitabh Bachchan's near fatal accident on the set in 1982.

WR: Yes, it was awful. Poor fellow. Thank God he recovered.

NMK: Manmohan Desai was an amazing man. I made a documentary on him in 1987, and was very fond of him. He had a beautiful singing voice.

WR: Really? I didn't know that. He would always be jumping about. He could never sit still.

As I told you, I have a logical mind and I would ask Manji how some situations in his films were possible. He would say: 'Waheedaji, it's a Manmohan Desai movie—there is no logic. No truth. No reality.'

I remember a scene in *Coolie* where the villain is chasing Amitabh, Chintu [Rishi Kapoor] and me. I fall and am injured, and a bandage is put on my forehead.

The next scene we were filming was the climax scene. We shot it somewhere near the Bandra Reclamation. A huge crowd had gathered to watch us shoot. Kadar Khan was also there and he was very popular too.

After a few shots, I said: 'These assistants are very bad. They should have remembered to put the bandage on my forehead for continuity. I should have thought of it myself.' Chintu looked at me and said softly: 'This must be the first time you're working with Manmohan Desai. There's nothing for you to worry about because he never gives the viewer the time to see what went wrong where. If you notice the continuity in his movie that means the picture is a flop.' *[we laugh]*

NMK: He was an original. I still miss him.

WR: He suffered from terrible backaches and poor health. Manji's passing was a loss to Hindi cinema and a big shock for us all. He had a great personality.

NMK: This is really the age of the celebrity. And thanks to Facebook and Twitter, everyone seems to want to know what the stars are doing on a daily basis. Before the Net, you must have had contact with your fans. Did you receive letters from your admirers? When did that start?

WR: Just after the release of *C.I.D.* I started getting fan mail. In the early days, I read the postcards and letters. I didn't have a secretary and so I threw away everything. I was told it was rude not to reply because most fans only wanted a signed photograph.

So I started sending out signed photographs.

I got strange fan mail too. There was a man who sent me eight-page letters every day for weeks on end. He wrote: 'I am going to build a Taj Mahal for you, better than the real one. You live in my heart . . .' He claimed to be an architect and I wondered if it was true and if so, how did he find the time to write such long letters to me? *[we laugh]*

NMK: Did you ever meet any of your fans?

WR: Yes, I did. A young man once wrote saying we did not need to marry because we were already married. Crazy fellow. I forgot all about it, but then one day he landed up at our door. It was very scary. Thankfully my sisters and my servants were there. When one of our servants tried to stop him from entering the house, he said: '*Tu kaun hai chaar paisewala, hato! Main apni biwi se milne aaya hoon.*' [Cheapskate! Who are you to stop me? I have come to see my wife.]

We had to call the watchman to get rid of him. It was a frightening experience.

NMK: I hope you have had a more positive encounter with a fan.

WR: I had a very special encounter once. One day a woman came up to me in a shop and said: 'I have wanted to meet you for years. I have something personal I want to share with you. You know Shanti, the character you played in *Trishul*? Well, my life was just like hers. I was in love with someone and was expecting his child. He abandoned me, but I decided to bring up the child on my own. It was a terrible struggle. When I saw you in *Trishul*, I thought to myself, if you could do it, so could I.' I found her story very moving.

NMK: The 1978 film you are talking about tackled a very daring subject because in those days the story of single mothers was uncommon in Hindi cinema and frowned upon by society. *Trishul* was a very popular Yash Chopra film based on a Salim–Javed script with some leading stars, including Amitabh Bachchan and Sanjeev Kumar.

WR: Yes, it was popular and it dealt with a bold subject. Unmarried mothers had to face many social stigmas. There is a famous scene in the film in which someone asks the hero Vijay, who is forever putting himself in danger, why he never fears anything in life and he answers: '*Maine maa ki nazron mein maut har din dekhi hai, to mujhe kis baat ka darr?*' [I have seen death in my mother's eyes every day. What could possibly frighten me now?]

Vijay finally has his revenge on his father by taking over his business and renaming the company 'Shanti' after his mother.

NMK: Before *Trishul* you played the heroine opposite Amitabh Bachchan. Was it odd to play the mother of an actor who was once your romantic lead?

WR: By the late 1970s, I had started playing mother roles. This kind of casting is not unusual in Indian cinema. Even in regional cinema, in Tamil and Telugu films, many actresses have played the heroine, mother and sister of the same male star. Audiences have never questioned it.

NMK: I can't imagine an actor playing Anushka Sharma's hero in one film and her father in another, even if the male star is old enough in real life to be her father. But ours is not to reason why. *[we laugh]*

Since you started working in Hindi films in 1955, you have seen the heroine's character change over the decades. How do you define this change?

WR: Every ten years you can see a distinct change in the role of the heroine. In the 1950s and '60s, the hero and heroine had more or less equal importance. You also had Meena Kumariji's many heroine-oriented films in the 1950s—the character she played won the sympathy of the audience because she was a woman who sacrificed everything in the name of love or family duty. People liked Meena Kumari in those roles.

In the 1970s, the hero took over and the violent action film became popular—that was Amitabh Bachchan's era. In his time, the girl became a kind of showpiece, that's all. The heroines had nothing to do. But I think roles for women are getting better again in Indian cinema.

NMK: Is there a character you would have liked to play?

WR: Radha in *Mother India* and the role Suchitra Sen played in *Mamta*. I liked the character of Radha because she made such a deep impact on the minds of people.

In fact, when producers wanted to cast me in a mother's role, to persuade me they would say: 'This is a *Mother India* role.' But it was not at all true!

We artistes are very greedy and want to be in the film from the first to the last frame. All artistes like the challenge of growing old on screen. It proves what great actors we are—how real we look at every age. *[we laugh]*

NMK: I was reading an article on Audrey Hepburn recently and her son Luca Dotti remembered her saying: 'I don't understand why people see me as beautiful.' It is an amazing and a heart-warming statement. The fact that Audrey Hepburn was not vain makes her even more beautiful.

How aware were you of being regarded as a great beauty?

WR: *[laughs]* I promise you no one ever told me: 'Wow, how beautiful you are!' They would say: 'You photograph well.' Therefore the compliment was directed at the photographer or the make-up artist or whoever.

I am being very honest with you and God knows it, I have never thought of myself as beautiful. I knew I had a photogenic face, but I've never thought I looked like Aishwarya Rai or Hema

167

Malini. People look at them and would say, 'Wow!' I didn't think I had a 'wow' kind of personality. When I see my photographs, I think I'm pretty but nothing special.

Now that I am older everyone tells me: 'You are very graceful.' I wonder why they did not say that before.

NMK: I can never forget the shot in *Pyaasa* at the end of the film when Vijay comes to ask you to go away with him. You stand at the balcony and look down and smile at him. You radiate such beauty. You also look exquisite in many films, including *Chaudhvin Ka Chand*.

WR: Really? Perhaps my leading men and directors were scared of telling me I was beautiful. But that's how it was and perhaps it was better that way.

NMK: There seems to be a greater emphasis on the physique of the actress today—she must be beautiful, slim, tall and glamorous. Was the look of the actress always that important?

WR: An actress has to be slim because the camera magnifies your size. You look much bigger than you are. The clothes the heroines wear today require the actresses to have good figures—many are former models or beauty queens.

NMK: It's interesting to note that actresses of your era often had a background in dance—in other words they brought skills of another discipline involving performance and rigorous training to the cinema—whereas actresses now often have a background in fashion and beauty contests.

But what is true is that actresses across generations have influenced fashion. I hear that was the case in your era too. Young women would ask their tailors to copy Nargis's blouses or Sadhana's kurtas. Did you start any fashion trend?

WR: I don't think my clothes were copied but my hairstyle was. I had a centre parting with two waves falling on either side of my forehead. My hair fell naturally like that. Nirupa Roy told me she tried to do her hair like mine. But her hairdresser said her forehead was broader and so it wouldn't work.

Whenever I had my hair done, the Chinese girls who worked at the parlour would say: 'Madam, everyone asks for the Waheeda Rehman cut.'

NMK: I was just reminded how rarely you see Chinese girls working in hair saloons in India any more! Wonder when that change happened.

You have worked with directors of all generations, including Aparna Sen in her 2005 film *15 Park Avenue*, which won a National Award. Was there any difference working with a woman director?

WR: There was no real difference, really. Aparna is a very clear and good director. She told me the story of the film over the phone and when I heard it, I immediately accepted the role. I liked the story and found it a strong subject. I played the mother of two daughters, one of whom suffers from schizophrenia. The reason why I agreed so readily to work with Aparna Sen was that I liked her earlier films. Both *36 Chowringhee Lane* with Jennifer Kendal and *Mr and Mrs Iyer* were good films.

NMK: Once again you played the mother in Rakeysh Mehra's *Rang De Basanti* and then in his *Delhi-6* you played the grandmother. How was the experience of working with him?

WR: Rakeysh first came to me for *Delhi-6*. He narrated the story but then he kind of vanished. Some years later, he came back to Bangalore to see me and said he wanted to narrate another idea and told me the story of *Rang De Basanti*. I didn't think I had much of a role in the film, but he insisted and said: 'Perhaps not in terms of screen time, but the mother is pivotal to the story and triggers the change in the main characters.' Rakeysh said if I did not accept the role, he would bring the whole unit to Bangalore, build the set on my farm and shoot.

When I was given the screenplay of *Rang De Basanti*, Rakeysh Mehra asked me to attend a workshop.

'Workshop? What workshop?'

'Waheedaji, have you never attended a workshop?'

I said we didn't have workshops in our time—no one did, not even Yash Chopra. I asked him to explain what a workshop was and he said the cast sat in a circle and read the lines out loud.

Aamir Khan and the whole jingbang, including Madhavan and Sharman Joshi, came for the workshop and when my turn came, I read the first two lines and then said: 'Blah, blah, blah.' They burst out laughing. I said the shoot was a month away, and it was too soon for me to memorize my lines.

Rakeysh's team was very dedicated. Aamir is a very professional kind of an actor. Like Amitabh, he takes his work very seriously. We also laughed and joked a lot during the making of the film.

NMK: *Rang De Basanti* had a big impact on young audiences.

WR: Yes, it did. I was coming out of a Bangalore hotel once, and the public relations girl stopped me and held my hand and said: '*Rang De Basanti* has had a huge effect on us all. It has woken us up. We're always blaming the system and the government, but we must ask ourselves how we as individuals can change things.'

It's good when a film brings about positive change.

NMK: Some people think that cinema has a bad influence too. Do you hear comments like that?

WR: Because of that brutal and horrific rape that happened in Delhi in December 2012, many people have said to me: 'It's because of your Bollywood.' What nonsense!

A few weeks ago some friends and I went to Cambodia and we saw several statues of topless women in the temples there. You mean to say if you see images of half-clad women, it encourages men to rape?

NMK: That sadistic rape and murder of the young Delhi girl, who came to be known as Nirbhaya, was the worst crime I have heard of in recent times.

It woke people up to the reality of violence against women. Attitudes have to change because rapes in India have not decreased in number. So many children are raped—it's beyond comprehension.

WR: It's completely horrifying. I hear that most rapes take place within the family—an uncle, a grandfather or else a neighbour. People say girls should not go out, but if this is happening within the home, what is a woman supposed to do? It is so deeply disturbing.

Parents and teachers must teach children correct values. The mindset has to change—and change soon.

NMK: Many people in films have spoken about the violence against women. Do you believe that artistes should have a sense of social responsibility?

WR: Yes, we must. I have been involved with social work for forty-five years and worked for the Bangladesh relief fund and collected funds for the War Widows Association, the Spastics Society and schools for the disabled. I have been a brand ambassador for Pratham, which works for underprivileged children in India. I continue to attend their events and dinners and lend them my support.

I used to feel awkward talking about my charity work. I didn't want people to think I was somehow showing off. Then a friend said it was silly to feel awkward because talking about it would help draw attention to the social cause.

My parents believed in social work. God has given us a lot. We should not be concerned only with our needs. There is only that much we need in life. We're capable of feeling the pain and suffering of others, and if we contribute even a little, it helps—a pond can be filled drop by drop.

NMK: You clearly have a deep sense of empathy for the plight of others. But what makes you angry or upset?

WR: I rarely get angry. But if I am angry—oh my God!

Sometimes halfway through a movie I realized that I made a bad mistake—that I should never have agreed to do this film in the first place—*that* has made me angry. When I realized too late it was the wrong role, the wrong unit and the wrong director. This kind of thing has upset me in the past, but I have never walked out of a film halfway. When it happened, I would come home from the shoot in a bad mood. I wouldn't talk to anyone. I'd go straight into my room, lock the door and stay there till dinner was served. I'd only come out to eat dinner and then immediately retreat into my room. My sisters would tell me to yell or shout—just as long as I said something.

I usually withdraw into myself when I feel angry or upset.

NMK: I am sure you can't tell me which film was the bad choice! But how do you let your anger out?

WR: I took it out on the screen. You know my directors always thought I was very delicate, but soon they realized that I have very strong hands. For a scene in *Reshma Aur Shera* I had to slap Amitabh, and for another in *Mujhe Jeene Do*, I had to slap Rajendra Nath. In each instance, after the shot was filmed, my co-stars told the directors that I should pretend to slap them and not actually do it. *[we laugh]*

NMK: Talking about something irritating—that's the wrong information on your Wikipedia page. Besides other errors, they have your birthday as 14 May 1936.

WR: Vinod Khanna sent me flowers on 14 May this year thinking it was my birthday. I had to explain to him I was born on 3 February 1938, and not in May and not in 1936. And I was not born in Hyderabad but in Chingleput, which is now called Chengalpattu, a suburb about sixty kilometres south of Madras. I am Tamilian and not a Hyderabadi, as many believe.

Wikipedia has the wrong day, year and place of birth.

Why can't they check? It's embarrassing. And this incorrect information gets printed elsewhere.

NMK: I agree such errors should be avoided.

You have had a long career in films, but unlike many actors who had to face years of struggle before becoming successful, you arrived in Bombay in 1955 with a contract waiting for you.

Nevertheless it took you almost eight years to buy your own home. How many times did you have to change homes in Bombay before that?

WR: Many times. When my mother and I first moved here, we stayed at the Norman Guest House on Marine Drive. Landlords were very scared to rent their flats to film people because film people had a reputation of not paying the rent on time nor vacating when they were supposed to. Thankfully my mother and I were not like that, and so we managed to find places to rent. We moved to a two-bedroom flat on 16th Road in Khar at the end of 1955 from the Norman Guest House. I can't remember the name of the building, but we lived there for about two years. That was the time when *C.I.D.* and *Pyaasa* were being made.

Our next home was a ground-floor flat at 57 Worli Sea Face. We stayed there for about a year. By the end of 1957, we moved to an apartment in Colaba near the Radio Club. You will remember my mother passed away there on 12 December

1957. After my mother died, Sayeeda and her family came to live with me.

From Colaba, we shifted to a fourth-floor apartment in Sea Bell on Nepean Sea Road and lived there from 1958 to 1962. While we were at Sea Bell, I noticed a new building called 'Poonam' that was being built opposite us. I thought I'd try and buy a ground-floor flat there. That was the first place that I bought. It became our home for ten years from 1962.

NMK: When did you move to your current home in Bandra?

WR: In 1972, I bought the ground floor of this bungalow. The original house had a huge garden, and the builder who owned the whole plot decided to build Galaxy Apartments in the compound. When it was ready, Salim Khan and his family moved here in the early 1970s. I wasn't married in those days and did not know Salim Saab but he made a courtesy call. And later I became close friends with his wife, Salma, and the whole family.

My upstairs neighbours are Sikander Fateh Ali—the cousin of Salim Ali, the famous birdwatcher—and his wife, Qamar. They thought our bungalow should have its own name, so we called it 'Sahil' [Shore].

NMK: Anyone passing your end of Bandstand will see many fans milling around the gates of Galaxy Apartments hoping to catch a glimpse of the superstar Salman Khan, entering or exiting. Galaxy Apartments has become famous.

WR: I have known Salman since he was ten years old. His father used to really scold the poor fellow! Salim Saab was very strict. He has three sons—Salman, Arbaaz and Sohail—and two daughters—Alvira and Arpita.

NMK: We have spoken a bit about your husband, Shashi Rekhy. But I'd like you to tell me more about him.

You acted together in the 1964 film *Shagoon*. I am not sure many people have seen the film, but they will remember the film's amazing songs by Sahir and Khayyam, including 'Parbaton ke pedon par' and 'Tum apna ranj-o-gham apni pareshaani mujhe de do'.

WR: We met on the sets of *Shagoon*. In the beginning I used to call him by his screen name, Kamaljeet, and sometimes just Kamal. When I got to know him better I called him by his real name, Shashi. He wasn't very well known and was a relative newcomer. By the 1960s, I was in a position to help newcomers and was open to the idea of working with new actors and directors. *Shagoon* was Nazar's first film as director. Before that he worked as Mehboob Saab's assistant on *Son of India* and that's how he knew Kamaljeet. As you know Mehboob Saab introduced Kamaljeet in *Son of India*.

Kamal was very shy and quiet. During the making of *Shagoon*, I sensed he was fond of me, but he said nothing. He sent me a big box of chocolates on Eid. My sisters and their children were living with me at the time and there were about fourteen or fifteen people in the house. When I saw the box, I said: 'How sweet of him to send chocolates for us.' My sister Sayeeda gave me a funny look and said: 'You fool! They are not for us, they're for you.' *[laughs]*

Sometime later Kamal sent me a tall candle. We sisters were very fond of food. We decided to make a soup and soufflé, switch off all the lights and have a candlelit dinner. We settled at the table, ready for our meal, and although we tried everything, the candle just would not light. I said jokingly: 'The candle is just like Kamal. Shy and reserved.'

NMK: How did *Shagoon* do at the box office?

WR: It flopped miserably; even *Son of India* had not done well and neither had his other films. When Kamal realized that in spite of working with Mehboob Saab, his career had not taken off, he thought it was better to give up acting and try something else. I think it was a very unusual decision because actors rarely want to quit.

Kamaljeet stopped working in films and went to London. I don't remember what he did there, but a year later, he moved to Toronto where some of his Delhi friends were living. He settled in Toronto and opened some shops. Every winter he would return to Delhi to meet his family.

NMK: What kind of business did your husband do?

WR: Shashi started exporting garments to Canada. He and his partner planned to open a restaurant in San Diego. But they had to put the idea on hold because Shashi needed to return to Bombay to oversee his garment factory as the production was not going well.

Whenever Shashi came to Bombay he stayed with his close friends Yash and Hiroo Johar. They happened to be close friends of mine, so the three of them would come over together. I knew Yash Johar from the days when he worked as production-in-charge on *Mujhe Jeene Do* and *Guide*. He was a very decent man.

One day when Yash and Hiroo had brought Shashi over, I noticed that he had put on a lot of weight since the *Shagoon* days, and I asked him jokingly: 'You must have a Punjabi wife who is feeding you parathas and ghee.' He laughed.

Sometime in 1972, I told him I wanted to open an Indian restaurant in Paris. Shashi said: 'You know my partner and I are planning to start a restaurant in San Diego—why don't we work together?' A few days later, Shashi called and said: 'I'd like to talk to you about something. Can I come over?'

I had this feeling he was very fond of me, but I thought he wanted to discuss my investing in a restaurant. I was keen on the idea of an Indian restaurant in Paris, but actually didn't have the money to invest at that time. I decided that I would be open with him and explain the situation when he came over.

As we were having coffee, Shashi suddenly said: 'I want to marry you. Will you marry me?' It hit me like a bombshell. Did

I hear right? I looked down. I didn't know what to say. He was quiet for a minute and then said: 'I asked you something. You didn't answer.' All I could say was that I needed time to think it over.

There comes a moment in life when we all think about settling down and having children. I was thirty-four, and to be very frank, my career was no longer at its peak because Hindi cinema as such does not have good roles for women over thirty. I wanted to get married and so I thought about his proposal.

Yash Johar used to call me 'Maalik'. A few days later, he called me and said: 'Maalik, you'll be the death of us. This fellow is pacing up and down the room, smoking like crazy. We live in a small flat and we're going to fall sick with all his smoke. Is it yes or no? I think you had better say yes. Shashi is a good man. I know him. You have worked with him.'

'Yes, I have, though I can't say I know him well.'

'He's good-looking and a man of good character.'

I thought about it for a few more days and then finally agreed to marry Shashi.

You may not know this, but I was engaged a year before that. My sisters were pressurizing me to marry and like a fool I agreed. I was engaged to someone from Najibabad in UP. I don't want to name him because it's not fair.

Things did not work out and I decided not to marry. When Shashi proposed to me, some friends advised me not to say yes in a hurry. But I have always taken risks in life and knew that Shashi was a decent man. I was comfortable in his company.

NMK: What kind of wedding ceremony did you have?

WR: A registrar marriage. We had to wait six weeks for a date from the registry office. Although we wanted to keep our wedding a private affair, the news somehow leaked out in the press. Sadhana called Yash Johar whom she considered a rakhi brother and said: 'What is this? Waheeda is getting married? I heard the news from a friend in New York.' Yashji pretended to be surprised: 'No! Really? To whom?' *[laughs]*

Shashi went into a panic and we decided to have a high-powered meeting at Yash Johar's house to discuss what we should do. There was Yash, Hiroo, my sisters, Shashi and I. Yash thought we should go to America and get married in Nevada. He had heard that one could marry there in twenty-four hours. I said no—how could I marry without my family? We even talked about having a kind of ceremony in which couples exchange garlands—the kind you see in the movies. But Shashi said: 'I'll only start laughing. I'll think we're shooting!'

Finally Yash said: 'Shashi, you don't follow any religion. At least Waheeda prays. Why not call a maulvi and have a nikah?' Shashi agreed and we had a Muslim wedding on 26 July 1974 in our Sahil home.

NMK: Did your husband's family have any problem with his marrying a Muslim?

WR: His brother and uncles were not at all religious. Shashi was

*Shashi Rekhy and Waheeda Rehman were married in Bombay on
26 July 1974. They first met on the sets of* Shagoon *in 1964.*

forty years old and had just announced that he was marrying
Waheeda. 'Which Waheeda?' They were very happy to hear it
was Waheeda Rehman.

Our wedding was a very small and quiet affair. We were
about sixty people—there was Shashi's family, my family and
our close friends, including Nanda, Hiroo Johar and Salim and
Salma Khan. There was no press at all. I was most upset that
Yash Johar was away in London on urgent work and couldn't
attend our wedding.

After Shashi and I were married, we moved permanently to
this house. Shashi got on very well with our neighbour Salim
Saab and so we were constantly at his place. We would sit on

the balcony and talk for hours. We met in good times and in bad times.

NMK: Did you live in Canada for any period of time?

WR: No, but we went to Toronto and San Diego for our honeymoon. I was in a hurry to have children and within six months, I was expecting. Shashi's mother was very pleased and, because her other son had not married, she asked us to stay in India. She wanted to be near her future grandchildren. My son Sohail was born in 1975 and daughter Kashvi in 1976.

NMK: Kashvi is an unusual name.

WR: It was Shashi's idea. He said if we had a daughter, we should call her Kashvi because he liked the name of Marlon Brando's former wife—Anna Kashfi.

I asked Ishaq Saab, who has recently been helping me brush up on my Urdu, the meaning of my children's names and he said: 'Sohail means a bright star in Arabic and Kashvi means a shining star in Sanskrit.'

NMK: Their names mean the same thing? What about Waheeda?

WR: It comes from the Arabic word '*wahid*', which means 'one'. Or you could say the only one.

NMK: The unique.

Can you tell me if there was any tension between you and your husband because you were a famous star? Was it awkward for him, for example, that you were recognized everywhere?

WR: No, to the contrary. If I happened to call someone for information and introduce myself as Mrs Rekhy, he would say: 'Don't waste time. Just tell them you're Waheeda Rehman. Your work will be done at once.' When I did that, I always got an enthusiastic response: 'Waheeda Rehman? You should have said so.' Shashi was very generous to think in that way.

NMK: Why did you move to Bangalore?

WR: The Bombay weather was a problem for Shashi. He found the humidity uncomfortable. His cousin who lived in Bangalore encouraged us to move there. One year we decided to go to Bangalore to celebrate our wedding anniversary, and Shashi fell in love with the climate. That's when we decided to settle down and live on a farm there. We ran a dairy and a vegetable farm, grew sunflowers and made sunflower oil.

In 1983, when we were about to leave Bombay, Yash Johar told me: 'Don't take all your belongings; you'll be back in six months. Maalik, you've worked for a long time in films. How can you live with your young children on a farm, in a jungle? You're crazy.'

At that time Shashi's brother had fallen very ill with cancer, and so he was rushed to New York where he spent months at Sloan–Kettering.

So the children and I moved to Bangalore when Shashi was away in New York. The farmhouse was not quite completed and we had to live in two rooms. The kitchen was ready, but there was no power. I remember the children had to do their homework by gaslight. But I was determined to move and once I decide something, I have to do it.

I wanted my children to grow up in a natural environment, for them to know the beauty of flowers, fruits, trees and animals. It was lovely and peaceful living on a farm. I enjoyed looking after it. I learned how to make paneer at home—how wonderful it was to pick your own vegetables and eat off the land.

We ended up living on the farm for sixteen years and only returned to Bombay in 2009.

NMK: What about your Bombay house?

WR: I rented it out and locked up a room for us to stay in whenever we came to visit. The room didn't have a kitchen, but Salim Saab was very kind to us and insisted on sending food every day. They sent us tons to eat!

Our garage had been converted into a gym that Salman uses. If I happened to arrive from Bangalore late at night and Salman saw me the next day, he would immediately ask: 'Aunty, have you had tea?' He would shout across to his flat in Galaxy

Aparments: *'Aarey nashta aur chai bhejo Aunty ke leeye.'* [Send tea and breakfast for Aunty.] He is very sweet.

NMK: I believe you made cereal in Bangalore.

WR: Yes, it was called Good Earth Breakfast Cereal. Somehow the idea of promoting it as my product embarrassed me. When I went to America to attend a charity gala and visit my niece, we saw Paul Newman's meat sauce bottles in a mall. My niece said: 'See? Paul Newman has his name and photograph on the bottle. He gives the money he earns to charity. If you can be a brand ambassador for other brands, why not promote your own cereal?' That's when we added my photograph on the box. A shopkeeper later told me everyone asked for Waheeda's cereal.

I must tell you about a funny incident. During the shooting of *Chandni*, Chintu [Rishi Kapoor] said: 'Arey, Waheedaji, you have started a serial? Where do you do the shooting?'

'Shooting? What shooting?' Then I realized what he meant. 'Chintu, I am making the eating kind of cereal, not a TV serial.'

NMK: When you moved to Bangalore, was it difficult adapting to your new life away from the glamour of films?

WR: I didn't miss acting very much. After we left Bombay, if I had agreed to act in a film, it was for financial reasons. I had some old income tax dues to pay, and so occasionally I accepted a mother's role.

With nieces and nephews at home at Poonam Apartments, Nepean Sea Road, Bombay. Circa 1965.

I always wanted to have children. I spent a lot of time with my nieces and nephews, so taking care of Sohail and Kashvi was nothing new to me.

NMK: Were you a strict parent?

WR: I was a little strict when my children were young. My mother was quite strict with us girls. I felt Shashi was too lenient. He said yes to everything that Sohail and Kashvi wanted. I don't believe in being rigid. That's too suffocating. You can break some rules, but discipline is still a good thing.

Now the children have grown up. We talk and fight too.

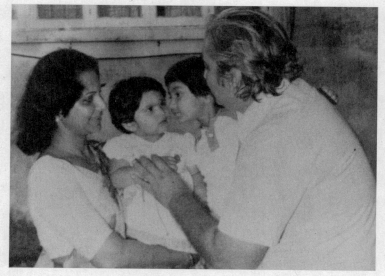

With (L to R) Kashvi, Sohail and her husband, Shashi Rekhy, on Kashvi's first birthday. Bombay, 1977.

They aren't scared of me any more. They know I am fine with whatever they choose to do, but I don't want an outsider telling me what they're up to. I always tell them: 'I may shout and scream at you, and even if I get angry, it will be for a short time. If you do something wrong, I am bound to get upset. But it doesn't mean you should not confide in me. I am your mother and am always there for you.'

Sohail and Kashvi live with me here at Sahil. They aren't married. You know nowadays young people talk of chemistry. I see many people divorcing around me, and so I don't force them to get married. I think they should just be happy and healthy.

NMK: Given the emphasis today on everyone looking young, especially celebrities, I am sure people have asked why you decided not to colour your hair.

WR: My mother did not have a single grey hair. My father turned grey young, and my sisters and I took after him. And because we were making films in colour in the 1970s, I had to start dyeing my hair.

In 1997, my husband had his first stroke. A week later my mother-in-law fell and broke her hip and needed hospitalization. There was chaos in the house—the kind of chaos they show in the movies. I remember once telling a producer: 'Why must you show tragedy after tragedy befalling the same family?' He smiled and said one day I would see that life could sometimes turn out like that. I realized he was right.

My husband was unwell, my cook had left, it was pouring cats and dogs, the car wasn't working as the brakes had failed, we had no electricity and, on top of all that, for two days the phone was out of order—disaster means *disaster*! I had to cook, look after my husband and run back and forth to the hospital, as my mother-in-law was frantically worried about Shashi.

There was no time to colour my hair and by the time things had settled down, my hair had turned grey. That's when I decided to stop colouring it. When I came to Bombay for the first time after that and my friends saw me, they looked shocked—Nanda, Salim Saab, everyone. I said my children were grown, and Shashi had silvery hair, so why not me?

Mrs Krishna Raj Kapoor saw me in a shop one day and was taken aback. She said: 'Waheeda, what have you done? I am so much older than you. Go straight to the saloon and get your hair dyed!' [*we laugh*]

Another funny thing happened. Sunil Dutt was in the ICU because he had suffered a stroke and was paralysed. He had been extremely helpful in getting my brother-in-law admitted to Sloan–Kettering in New York. Sunil Dutt knew everyone there because that's where Nargisji was treated for cancer.

When I entered his room in the hospital, and Sunilji saw me all grey, he was startled and said: 'Waheedaji, what's wrong? Shall I call the nurse? Why have you turned grey all of a sudden?'

'It didn't happen all of a sudden. I just stopped dyeing my hair. That's all. You're a grandfather now and we aren't young any more.' He laughed.

Nargis and Sunil Dutt were a wonderful couple. We were very close. We travelled together for charity shows and spent weeks together.

Once Nargisji and I went to London to attend a film festival. We were staying at the Hilton Hotel and would party till three in the morning. She would then call me early the next day and tell me to get ready quickly so we could go to Selfridges and Harrods for shopping. The person who looked after us in London, S.N. Gourisaria, kept complaining: 'It's 8.30 in the morning and you want to go shopping? I have to go to the office. You crazy people.'

With Nargis and Sunil Dutt at the Delhi premiere of Reshma Aur
Shera. *Delhi, 1971.*

NMK: S.N. Gourisaria? He's over eighty-five now and is living
between London and Calcutta. He used to organize the first
Indian film festivals in London in the late 1950s. He was well
known to everyone in the film industry, including Raj Kapoor,
Guru Dutt and Lata Mangeshkar.

Losing friends like Nargisji and Sunil Dutt must have been
terrible. You also had to bear the loss of your husband. Was he
ailing for a long time?

WR: Shashi was very careless about his health. He didn't believe
in doing any physical exercise. He never walked nor was he

careful about his diet. He would eat ghee and malai and meat—you know, very rich food.

As I told you, he had his first stroke in Bangalore in 1997. We rushed him to the hospital, which was far away from the farm. The doctors would not come to the house.

Sometime later when I came to Bombay for a visit, I discovered Lilavati Hospital was only five minutes away from our Bandra house. But Shashi did not want to move back. I told him it was very important we live near a hospital and doctors. Specialists in Bombay make home visits and that was reassuring.

Shashi was unwell much of the time. He was diabetic and his sugar count would get very high. He had high blood pressure and smoked very heavily too. We had a big argument. I said: 'No, sorry, I can't do this. We have to move.' The children were studying abroad and I was all alone. Very reluctantly he agreed to move back here. We had no choice really.

Between 1997 and 2000, he was admitted into the ICU several times, after suffering minor strokes. The first time he had a stroke, it had affected his speech, but gradually he regained normal speech. He became increasingly withdrawn and depressed. He started saying things like: 'My time is up, I'll go.' I felt very bad and tried to persuade him not to think such thoughts.

Kashvi was in America and wanted to get a job there. I was worried that Shashi would overhear us if we spoke over the phone, so I wrote her a letter asking her to come home. I told her that her father was missing her and kept saying that his time was up. My daughter came back to Bombay and exactly a month later, Shashi passed away. He died of a brain haemorrhage. He was only sixty-seven.

NMK: When was that?

WR: In November 2000. How time passes.

I don't like dwelling on sadness. I try to face difficult times and live through them. I accept the things that happen in life. We all have to deal with loss. What choice do we have?

NMK: Since your husband passed away, have your friends become a great support to you?

WR: I didn't have friends in my childhood because I was always unwell. Also, my father kept getting transferred from one city to another, so by the time we settled somewhere and made friends at the local school, we were on the move again. As a result, I didn't have close friends. I had my sisters, and probably that's the reason why I didn't miss not having friends.

After my mother passed away in 1957, my sister Sayeeda got divorced and she and her three children came to live with me. Then unfortunately Bi-Apa, who was in Pakistan, lost her husband. He died of cancer. He was only forty. So she returned to India with her family and stayed with me for a while. The house was always full.

But friends have become increasingly important to me over the years. Nanda is a close friend. We both read a lot and sometimes we sit together and imagine adapting a novel into a film. We discuss who could play the lead roles—Ashok Kumar? Rekha? We never cast each other.

NMK: When did you first meet Nanda?

WR: Before working together in *Kala Bazar*, we happened to see each other in some studio. She was with her mother. She told me later that she had smiled at me but I didn't smile back. I hadn't actually seen her.

Close friend Nanda was among the sixty guests at her private wedding ceremony held at Sahil in Bandra. 1974.

A few days later when the filming of *Kala Bazar* had started, I asked her to have lunch with me. She was a little surprised because she thought I had ignored her the previous time we met, but she agreed to join me. After that we had lunch together every day. I told her she was welcome to use the bathroom that was attached to my make-up room any time she wanted. We soon became very good friends.

Once, Nanda, her brother, my sister, some friends and I went on a holiday to Kodaikanal. From there we decided to go to Munnar in Kerala because we heard it was a very beautiful place.

Munnar was indeed lovely with flowing streams and green and lush tea estates. We were very keen to stay overnight. We found an English club that was run by a strange, rather scary-looking caretaker. He was dark-skinned and wore crisp white kurtas. We asked him if we could stay the night. He said there weren't enough rooms for us all, but if the women slept in the main building of the club and the men in the annex, we could manage somehow.

Nanda is very timid, so she became very suspicious. She wondered why the caretaker wanted the men to sleep in the annex and us women elsewhere. I reassured her and said there was nothing to worry about. So we went to the market and bought lungis and men's shirts to wear for the night, as we had no fresh clothes with us for the next day.

Nanda and I shared a room. She went in to have her bath and when she came out of the bathroom, she screamed on seeing the window of our bedroom wide open. I told her that I had opened the window because we needed fresh air. She said nothing doing and banged it shut. She was absolutely convinced that the caretaker would sneak into our room in the middle of the night through the window. It took some time before I could convince her not to worry about the poor fellow because he was unlikely to do us any harm. *[laughs]*

Nanda and I had some crazy times together.

NMK: Have you always had the same group of friends?

WR: Yes, more or less. We're a close-knit group of six women: Nanda, Asha Parekh, Sadhana, Helen, Shammi Rabadi and I. We meet often and do things together. Last year Asha, Helen and I went to Turkey for a holiday. Asha and I went to Kutch for a few days after that.

I also used to meet Shakila and Jabeen very often. Jabeen acted in *Taj Mahal* with Bina Rai and in James Ivory's *The Householder*. She didn't become a big star. I met Shakila during the making of *C.I.D.* She was the heroine and I played the vamp. We don't see each other as often nowadays.

NMK: How did you get to know Helen?

WR: Helen and I performed a dance together in a film called *Baazi*, which was made in 1968. Dharmendra was the leading man. We didn't become friends at the time, but when Salim Saab and Helen got married he would bring her over to

Accompanying Helen (left) and Asha Parekh on holiday in Istanbul, Turkey. May 2012. Photograph: Waheeda Rehman.

With friends (L to R) Jabeen, Shakila and Nanda. Shakila was the leading lady in Waheeda Rehman's first Hindi film, C.I.D.

our place very often. We soon became close friends. Helen was also very close to Nanda because they had made many movies together over the years.

Asha Parekh and I have not worked in the same film but I used to meet her at various parties and premieres over the years. About ten years ago, she came to Bangalore to shoot a TV serial called *Baaje Payal* which was produced by Shammi Rabadi and Asha. The serial was about dancers. Since Shammiji and I were old friends, I got to know Asha very well.

And there's Sadhana whom I met during the making of a film called *Ulfat*. I told you that was an unreleased film of mine; Raaj Kumar was also acting in it. Shashi knew Sadhana's husband, Nayyar Saab, before he became a producer/director.

Sadhana and Nayyar Saab, Yash and Hiroo, and Shashi and I would get together very often. Then Nayyar Saab passed away.

NMK: What about friends unconnected to films?

WR: I have other friends who have nothing to do with films, including Barota. Her husband, Jayant Malhotra, was an industrialist and they were Shashi's close friends too. Other dear friends are Harish Salve, the son of the former Union minister N.K.P. Salve, and his wife, Meenakshi, who is a relative of Shashi's. They live in Delhi and whenever they come to Bombay, they come over to the house for a meal. Indira Jaising is someone I am very fond of. She is the assistant solicitor general of India and lives near me in Bandra.

I met Kiran Mazumdar-Shaw and her husband, John, thirty years ago when she was just starting her company. We've been good friends ever since that time. She is a down-to-earth and compassionate person.

It's good to know people who are not working in films, otherwise the conversation tends only to be about the movies and it's not exciting to talk about films all the time.

You know, I am amazed how fascinated people are by Indian cinema. Oh my God, are they crazy about films!

NMK: Do you think this interest is greater than before?

WR: Yes, I think so.

NMK: You have met countless people in your life—do you find people interesting?

WR: I think people are very interesting. They have such individuality—their habits and ways of thinking. I like analysing people and I like analysing my own behaviour too. I am curious to know why a person speaks or behaves in the way he or she does. I don't like generalizing, nor am I judgemental in any way, but it's fascinating to see how different people react in different situations.

I am a good listener. I try not to react instantly. If someone doesn't smile back at me, I assume that there must be something on their mind or perhaps something is troubling them. I don't take it personally and jump to conclusions. Either way, I don't believe everyone should like me. Why should they?

Even in a marriage, one should not take the other for granted. One has to accept and respect the individual.

NMK: What about the other people who have shared your life? I am sure members of your staff have worked with you and your family for many years.

WR: My driver Naseer lives in Bangalore now. He has been with me for forty years. He was a young boy when he first started working for me. He was the same age as a nephew of mine. When he first arrived, he proudly told me he was previously working for the spiritual head of the Bohras.

Naseer is married and is old now. He's got diabetes and can't see properly, but refuses to wear specs. The poor fellow has lost most of his teeth. He is very reliable. He's a sweet and sincere man.

My children argue about who will keep Naseer after I am gone. It's not as though he can work any more. He is retired and lives in our rented place in Bangalore.

There was another boy, Raju, who was about fourteen or fifteen when he started working in the fields on our Bangalore farm. Raju slowly learned how to cook and became the house cook. He has been with us for thirty years. He's married and has children.

NMK: I am sure many young women who aspire to become actresses would appreciate your advice on acting. What is the most important thing when approaching a role?

WR: They have to understand the kind of role they're playing. Who is the character? No matter how much you learn about the techniques of acting, unless you put your soul into it, it will not make any impression. Your soul has to be there for any sincerity to come through.

When my guru T.M.S. Pillai was teaching me Bharatanatyam in Chennai, he sat me down one day and said: 'I have taught you everything, the mudras, the bhavas. But your facial expressions are the most important thing and that is where your soul is visible. No guru in the world can teach you that.'

I had no training in acting, but even if you are a trained actor, I know you have to put that little bit of soul into your performance—and that can only happen when you have understood the character perfectly and what is required in this moment, in this scene.

NMK: What do you mean by 'soul'?

WR: Feeling the emotions totally. To imagine: if I were that person in that situation, how would I feel? If the character is a Shankar or a Vijay, a little bit of Dilip Kumar or Amitabh has to come into the character.

NMK: Is there always a bit of you in your characters?

WR: A little bit, but not too much. If there is too much then you're not acting—you are Waheeda all the time. You have to change yourself to become another character, but you do need to add your own emotions and personality.

What you bring to a character is a fine balance between craft and personality. But craft alone will not help you.

NMK: I am sure aspects of your personality are present in the different characters you have played. Which character is close to the real Waheeda Rehman?

WR: There's a bit of me in Shanti, Gulaabo and Rosie. But I think I am most like Rosie. She's a straightforward woman who knows her own mind. She stands by what she believes in.

NMK: If you hadn't become an actress, what would you have liked to be?

WR: When we were young, medicine was regarded as the only respectable profession for women. I always wanted to work, and I told my father I wished to become a doctor. He said: '*Beta*, you won't be able to study because of your poor health. How will you become a doctor?' I insisted that I would somehow. I'm still fascinated by medicine and homeopathy.

President V.V. Giri awards the Padma Shri to Waheeda Rehman in 1972. She went on to receive the Padma Bhushan, one of India's highest civilian awards in 2011.

There's a funny story I must tell you. When my father was alive, we had three peons who came from his office to help out in the house. One of the peons once told me that he had a bad headache. I made him a paste of coconut oil and talcum powder and asked him to apply half the paste on his temple and eat the other half. My sisters said: 'Are you crazy? Supposing something terrible happens to him?' I reassured them by saying: 'I am giving it to him with love and faith; nothing bad will happen.' I was very young.

NMK: Talcum powder?

WR: Yes! He applied the paste to his temple and ate the rest. Call it faith or whatever, but the peon later told me: 'God bless you, my headache has gone.' After that if he didn't feel well, he used to come to me for treatment.

I used to read all those Hamdard Dawakhana magazines. Hakims say 50–70 per cent of medicine can be found in your kitchen cabinet—turmeric, cloves, cinnamon and dry ginger. All these spices have medicinal properties.

My husband had a terrible cough once and I gave him some haldi mixed in milk. It is a common remedy. At first Shashi refused, but later he drank it. He said it had helped him. He once told me: 'Look, your Jesus Christ syndrome of healing people could end in tears. Some day you'll kill someone and then you'll hold your head in your hands and cry. Stop doing all this.' *[laughs]*

Shashi and I had a good marriage.

NMK: It sounds like you and your husband laughed a lot together. Now if you need to talk through important decisions, who do you turn to? Your son, Sohail? Or Kashvi?

WR: Sohail and Kashvi are young. I don't discuss my problems with my sisters either and never have. Sayeeda lives in Bombay, but goes to Panchgani often because her daughter Samina is studying there. Bi-Apa lives in Hyderabad and comes here to see her children who are now grown up. Sha-Apa lives between Kumbakonam and Hyderabad. My sisters keep travelling. What else can they do at this age?

I know they have their own problems. Why burden them with mine? When you believe in God, you hold His hand and leave it to Him to sort things out.

NMK: So you're not a worrier?

WR: No. When my husband and I moved to Bangalore, we were faced with many problems regarding our farmland. Shashi smoked heavily, and when he was worried, he smoked even more. I would try to calm him down and say: 'Leave it to God. Go to sleep. Tomorrow we'll see what can be done.'

And he would say, 'You're a Muslim, so you believe in the greatness of Allah and you leave everything in His hands.' Shashi liked my attitude, but, oh my God, did he worry! *[smiles]*

Wonderful memories shared with Shammi and Nargis during the making of Reshma Aur Shera. *Photographed in a tent in Jaisalmer by Nargis's nephew Sarwar Hussain. 1971.*

NMK: Many people with whom you have worked, and have been close to, have passed away in recent years. It must be very difficult to see your world disappearing around you.

WR: It is very difficult. I was recently asked to unveil Dev Anand's statue. It will be placed on Bandstand in Bandra. I felt very emotional. To think I had worked with him in my first Hindi film and there I was unveiling his statue. I couldn't stop myself from crying.

NMK: I was at that event and I could see you were very upset.
Bette Davis said something very wise: 'Old age isn't for

wimps.' What do you think are the good and bad things about getting older?

WR: One is more mature and patient. I think I am more understanding. I take life as it comes. I know everyone has problems—financial, emotional or health related. But when I am faced with problems, I try not to push them away. I think of ways of solving them.

I am not young any more. I am in a hurry to travel and see new places. I love travelling and taking photographs. Last year I went to London with Barota and we bought an Oyster card and sometimes travelled around by bus. If an Indian couple happened to be on the bus they would recognize me. I think Barota felt bad that Waheeda was seen roaming around in a London bus. But I don't mind. What's the big deal?

NMK: You must have heard this question a hundred times before, but do you have a favourite film?

WR: How strange! While we were having lunch today, Sohail and Kashvi asked me this very question. I said my top favourite is *Gone with the Wind*. My second favourite is *Legends of the Fall*—the one with Brad Pitt. I just love that film and don't mind seeing it again and again. I think Brad Pitt was very good.

There are many Hindi films that I have liked. The ones that stand out now are the old *Andaz, Mother India, Mughal-e-Azam, Sujata* and *Do Bigha Zamin*.

Among the recent films I like Imtiaz Ali's *Jab We Met*. I watch it again whenever it is on television. Kashvi always says: 'Mummy, think of your age.' So what? What has age got to do with it? I think it is a sweet and charming love story.

NMK: For actors who are immortalized on the screen ageing can be nevertheless difficult to accept.

WR: One must accept.

A long time ago when my eyes were getting weak, I had to wear reading glasses. In those days there was only one airline, Indian Airlines, and the flights would often get delayed, so I would always carry a book with me. One day Dev happened to see me reading in the airport lounge and said: 'Waheeda, why have you got your specs on?'

'Because I can't read without them.'

'That's not the point! Why can't you pretend you're reading?'
[we laugh]

NMK: You have known fame since 1955, when you first appeared in *Rojulu Marayi*. Did you find managing stardom over the years a difficult thing?

WR: It is difficult being famous, especially if you become well known overnight. Suddenly all India knows you, all Asia knows you, and even people abroad know who you are. You're on a high. Wherever you go, people want to meet you and know you.

You have attention, glamour, popularity and money. One film is enough for the world to know who you are. And sometimes it has nothing to do with talent.

Success in any field can change a personality. Maybe it did not affect me because my upbringing was very grounded. When we were growing up, I saw powerful army generals with cars and jeeps and everyone saluting them. But the moment they retired, no one bothered about them. They had to live in small flats and all that *shaan-baan* was gone.

I have always believed fame is here today and gone tomorrow. Who pays attention to you when you're old? Everything is ultimately transitory.

We actors are popular, and so, to some extent, we're forced to be artificial. Some of us do get cut off from reality. I accept I am getting old. I can't turn the clock back. But would I now be asked to play a character like Rosie? No. Could I do the snake dance now? No.

NMK: Starting as a teenager, you worked in the best Hindi films, and continued to have a hugely succesful career for over five decades. You have an army of fans and are deeply respected for your talent, integrity and grace. But it seems like you never fell for the illusion that fame would last. Am I right?

WR: No, it doesn't last.

I have believed in improving myself as a person, to keep learning. My curiosity has kept me alive. There was a time when I suddenly got the urge to paint. I went on the Net and tried to look for a teacher, but had no luck. I happened to meet Srilekha, my neighbour Sikander Fateh Ali's daughter-in-law, and asked her to find me an art teacher. She is an artist and, very sweetly, she brought me some paints, a brush and a drawing book. She told me to first train my hand by drawing. It was very kind of her.

I have a positive attitude to life and am peaceful in myself. I don't like to dwell on problems and negative thoughts. I get up at six, meditate for half an hour, do a bit of exercise, have my coffee and read the papers. I walk up and down the corridor in my house for a bit and then call my sisters, or someone may call me for a chat. I have my bath and get ready for the day. But if you asked me what I do every day to get so busy, I couldn't tell you. I am just very busy. Thank God.

NMK: Do you think much about the past?

WR: I don't like thinking about the past. But when I do, I think about the beautiful things that have happened—the wonderful moments of my childhood and the things that my parents would tell me.

I don't honestly believe in living in the past. It is the present that counts. I don't think about the future either. Maybe that's what gives me a sense of peace. I don't worry about what will happen tomorrow. That just isn't me.

With her son, Sohail, and daughter, Kashvi, at a recent function in Delhi where Waheeda Rehman was honoured as one of the twenty-five global Indians. Photograph courtesy: Taj Palace, Delhi.

APPENDIX

FILMOGRAPHY

YEAR	FILM	ROLE
1955	*Rojulu Marayi*	Dancer
1955	*Kaalam Mari Pochu*	Guest Appearance in the song 'Yeru thooki povayae annae chinnanae'
1955	*Alibabavum 40 Thirudargalum*	Dancer
1955	*Jayasimha*	Princess
1956	*C.I.D.*	Kamini
1957	*Pyaasa*	Gulaabo
1958	*12 O'Clock*	Bani Choudhary
1958	*Solva Saal*	Laajwanti
1959	*Kaagaz Ke Phool*	Shanti

YEAR	FILM	ROLE
1960	*Kala Bazar*	Alka
1960	*Ek Phool Char Kaante*	Sushma
1960	*Chaudhvin Ka Chand*	Jameela
1960	*Girl Friend*	
1961	*Roop Ki Rani Choron Ka Raja*	
1962	*Sahib Bibi Aur Ghulam*	Jabba
1962	*Bees Saal Baad*	Radha
1962	*Baat Ek Raat Ki*	Neela/Meena
1962	*Rakhi*	
1962	*Abhijan*	Gulaabi
1963	*Mujhe Jeene Do*	Chamelijaan
1963	*Kaun Apna Kaun Paraya*	Asha
1963	*Ek Dil Sao Afsane*	Sunita
1964	*Kohra*	Rajeshwari
1964	*Shagoon*	
1964	*Majboor*	Sushila Mehta
1965	*Guide*	Rosie Marco/Miss Nalini
1966	*Teesri Kasam*	Hirabai
1966	*Dil Diya Dard Liya*	Roopa
1967	*Patthar Ke Sanam*	Taruna
1967	*Ram Aur Shyam*	Anjana
1967	*Palki*	Mehroo

Appendix: Filmography

YEAR	FILM	ROLE
1967	*Ghar Ka Chirag*	
1968	*Neel Kamal*	Rajkumari Neel Kamal/ Sita
1968	*Aadmi*	Meena
1968	*Baazi*	
1969	*Khamoshi*	Nurse Radha
1969	*Shatranj*	Meena Thakur
1969	*Meri Bhabhi*	Maya
1970	*Prem Pujari*	Suman Mehra
1970	*Man Ki Aankhen*	Guddi (Geeta)
1970	*Dharti*	Jwala/Princess Chitralekha
1970	*Darpan*	Madhvi
1971	*Man Mandir*	Krishna and Radha
1971	*Reshma Aur Shera*	Reshma
1972	*Zindagi Zindagi*	Meeta Sharma
1972	*Trisandhya*	Indu
1972	*Subha-o-Sham*	Shirin
1972	*Dil Ka Raaja*	Laxmi
1973	*Phagun*	Shanta Bangan/ Shamrao Dhamle
1973	*Justice*	
1974	*Bangaru Kalalu*	
1976	*Aadalat*	Radha

Appendix: Filmography

YEAR	FILM	ROLE
1976	*Kabhi Kabhie*	Anjali Malhotra
1978	*Trishul*	Shanti
1979	*Aaj Ki Dhara*	
1980	*Jyoti Bane Jwala*	Malti
1980	*Jwalamukhi*	Savita Devi
1982	*Sawaal*	Anju D. Mehta
1982	*Namak Halaal*	Savitridevi
1982	*Namkeen*	Jugni (Jyoti)
1982	*Dharam Kanta*	Radha Singh
1983	*Himmatwala*	Savitri
1983	*Mahaan*	Janki
1983	*Coolie*	Salma
1983	*Pyaasi Aankhen*	
1983	*Ghungroo*	Rani Maa
1984	*Sunny*	Gayatri Inderjeet
1984	*Mashaal*	Sudha Kumar
1984	*Maqsad*	Sharda
1986	*Singhasan*	Rajmata Vardhan
1986	*Allah-Rakha*	Advocate Salma Anwar
1989	*Chandni*	Mrs Khanna
1991	*Lamhe*	Dai Jaan
1991	*Swayam*	
2002	*Om Jai Jagadish*	Saraswati Batra

YEAR	FILM	ROLE
2005	*Water*	Bhagavati (Narayan's Mother)
2005	*Maine Gandhi Ko Nahin Mara*	Principal Khanna
2005	*15 Park Avenue*	Meethi's Mother
2006	*Rang De Basanti*	Ajay's Mother
2006	*Chukkallo Chandrudu*	Arjun's Grandmother
2009	*Delhi-6*	Dadi (Annapurna Mehra)

INDEX

Index